To Janet Kuah ~

You have been an
abundant help to
me already in the few
times I've spoken with you.
If we ever get everything
in a row, I definitely
want Starr * Toof to do my
next books (because of
you). You are so kind and
helpful and just plain nice.

I wish for you everything
wonderful & beautiful moments
galore.

all the best,

Carol Fitzgerald

Embracing Beautiful Moments

Secrets To Enjoying Your Life!

A Book About the Delicate Art
of Enhancing Everyday Ways

Carol Fitzgerald

The Carobi Five Publishing Group
Naples ◆ 1994

—————➤•◦•◄—————

Published by
The Carobi Five Publishing Group
3106 Tamiami Trail North, Suite #275
Naples, Florida 33940

Copyright © 1991, 1994 by Carol Fitzgerald

Cover design by Alyce Mathias
Jacket & Author Photograph by Ed Chappell

Library of Congress Cataloging-in-Publication Data

Fitzgerald, Carol.
    Embracing beautiful moments: secrets to enjoying your life/by
Carol Fitzgerald.
    p. cm.
    Includes index
    1. Conduct of life. 2. Self-help techniques. 3. Happiness.
4. Interpersonal relations. I. Title.
BJ1581.2.F58 1994   177
                                    QBI94-1803

Library of Congress Catalog Card Number 94-072050
ISBN 0-9641596-0-0

Printed in the United States of America

Distributed by Baker and Taylor
Book Distributors

Also available through
book and gift specialty stores

Notice: Every effort has been made to locate the copyright owners of the material used in this book. Please let us know if an error has been made, and we will make any necessary changes in subsequent printings.

For Bill
Who has always allowed me to be me

For Patrick
Keri
Daniel
William
Mary Carol
Who taught me to be flexible

For My Mother and Father
Josephine and Alex
Who showed me the way

CONTENTS

INTRODUCTION

Dear Reader:

A perfect life? No such thing! Unfortunately, no one is immune to life's difficulties. A myriad of uncontrollable circumstances such as illnesses, abuses, alcoholism, drug problems, despair, depression, grief, death, devastating divorces, financial loss, homosexuality and a host of other unwanted, uninvited ills converge upon us everyday.

Though it's not always possible to change what happens to us, it *is* possible to change our response. Despite the have nots and any pain or unhappiness you may suffer, you can still live reasonably happy by seeking joy and by embracing life one beautiful moment at a time.

We must keep on "keepin' on". No matter what confronts us, we can whine and be negative, or we can put one foot in front of the other and look for joy. As one author put it: "We can count blessings, or we can count calamities. We can count blessings, or we can count life's blows and burdens." We choose.

When we think of beauty, outer beauty usually comes to mind. In order to achieve a balance between inner and outer beauty, we must weave the two together. Though outer beauty fades with age, inner beauty can be timeless. If we want it, we can cultivate and nurture and truly let it grow within us.

Neglecting our inner selves eventually leads to a negative outer self. If we look for the good and surround ourselves with people who have inner beauty, chances are we'll know peace. Important is to like yourself. When you do, you will have discovered one of the qualities of inner beauty: self-confidence.

You'll know because you'll walk straighter, you'll smile more and you'll think more about others and less of yourself. You will *feel* good. If you follow this: *Pretty is as pretty does,* thinking beautifully will result in being beautiful.

You will find ways within these pages to enhance your life and yourself, ways to cultivate beauty both inner and outer, ways to make your life a bit easier and ways to find joy.

Feel free to use whatever applies to give yourself a lift.

———➤•◄———

Part One

Much Ado About Being

———➤•◦•◄———

This section, the longest, is filled with giving and doing. That is, how to make others, including yourself, feel important. In it you will find:

Ideas for spreading joy
Special outings and projects for yourself
   and your family
Unique notions and ways of gift-giving
Ways of being kind and gracious
Many examples of nice gestures and letting
   people know you care

Also included are suggestions on:
calling cards
fragrances
flowers
activities
courtesies
writing letters
thank you notes

Generally how to give a little differently, do a bit more than the average, and be a tad better.

———➤•◦•◄———

Some ideas for cultivating inner beauty:
- ❤ Think happy thoughts
- ❤ Be grateful
- ❤ Be gracious
- ❤ Develop a positive attitude
- ❤ Grab some quiet time
  (relax and meditate)
- ❤ Be good to your body;
  it can affect your mind
- ❤ Be good to your mind;
  it can affect your body

Keeping in touch. Keep a calendar and make a point to remember the birthdays, anniversaries and other special days of your friends and relatives. Send them greeting cards or your own handwritten notes. Tuck in your children's school pictures, and other items of interest such as newspaper/magazine articles you feel they would find informative. I frequently clip jokes, unusual information or brainteasers and send them to my children, my nephews, other youngsters, and my mother and father. My aim is to put a smile on their face.

Remember his relatives. Write or call his parents as you do your own. Just to let them know how you and the children are and for general chit chat. Or send greeting cards and photos from time to time. Remember their birthdays and anniversaries, too. They'll be delighted that you stay in touch. Most men don't take the time to do this. Thoughtful wives and mothers do.

Walk your guests to the door when they leave. See your spouse and children out as well. Tell them to have a good day, or remind them that you love them.

If you're not in the shower or otherwise indisposed, get up from whatever you are doing and greet your family when they come in, too.

"The only way to have a friend is to be one," says Emerson. Reach out and be the kind of friend to others that you would like to have.

A train journey. Once, I wanted to jaunt aboard a train. I wanted to go far enough away that I could sleep in a berth. You know, those private little rooms you see in old movies? I wanted to sense the gentle rumble. Hear the clickety-clack, clickety-clack. I wanted to watch the land slide by. I wanted to experience a luxury of days gone by. So, one day we took a long weekend. My husband and at the time our four children. We rode the rails from Washington, D. C. to Orlando, Florida. What is there about riding on a train that gives you a special sense of wonder? Crisp white tablecloths, fresh flowers, sterling silver and white gloved waiters all added up to an exciting new experience for the children. If you want to lift your life above the ordinary, do journey aboard a train.

Edna St. Vincent Millay sums it up this way: "My heart is warm with the friends I make, And better friends I'll not be knowing; Yet there isn't a train I wouldn't take, No matter where it's going."

Pay compliments. My good friend, Lynn, held a going-away dinner for me when I was moving out of state. She asked guests to make a comment or two about me. My mother-in-law, Grace, looked over at me warmly, smiled and said, "Well, I don't know if Carol has learned anything from me during the past twenty years I've known her. But I have certainly learned a lot from her." That, to me, was one of the highest compliments I could have received.

Be sincere, but tell your family and friends when you notice something nice about them. Sometimes a compliment can be the start of a new friendship. Mine with Patricia started with just such a compliment. I noticed and made mention of something she wore, as we, total strangers, stood in line together at a school function once. We struck up a conversation: talked all the way to the punch bowl, all the way out of the cafeteria, down the hall and to our cars. One small compliment sparked what is today a dear friendship, a precious friendship, that began when I was very new in town. It remains so today.

Bake extra. When you bake, double or triple the recipe. This doesn't work with all recipes; you'll have to experiment to find out. Save some for another meal on a busy day or give one to a friend or neighbor. I often do this. In fact, when throwing a surprise 50th birthday party for my husband, I baked his birthday cakes (one doubled in a large pan and two regular 9 x 13 sizes) in his presence, with nary a suspicion on his part. You see, it wasn't anything out of the ordinary for him to see me bake in such quantities.

A fond custom. When a neighbor gives you a food item in a returnable container, rather than return it empty, why not go one step further and send it back with a cake or some cookies or a package of notecards or a new magazine. Got the idea? I saw my mother do this regularly. I welcomed a neighbor's visiting relatives with a dish of brownies one day. The following week they sent over a huge bowl of rice pudding for my family and me. I returned their bowl with a loaf of peach bread in it. Another time a friend returned a dish in which I'd brought dinner when she moved into her new home. In it she had placed a jar of homemade bread and butter pickles with a note: "My Mom taught me never to return a dish empty, so please enjoy the pickles. They're just a token of my thanks and appreciation for the dinner you brought over...." When I returned a pan with a homemade cake in it to Patricia and her family, her mother said, "I thought Carol was Italian. This is an Irish custom." Well, I don't know who invented the idea; it's probably just old-world hospitality, but I like it. And so do people I know who do the same.

Christmas cards. Each year, as the Christmas cards and photos arrive, I choose a spot, reach for my letter opener and read through them all. Well after Christmas, sometimes as late as February or March, I sit down again and re-read all of the notes and letters savoring them in a peaceful, quiet moment. Then I sort through each card, keeping the ones that give me true visual enjoyment. I use a pinking shears to pink the edges and voila! these become my gift tags for the following year's presents. Then, I put all of the photos in an album. The family photos we receive year after year hold their own pages in my album and at one glance, I see how they have all changed and grown. A special part of the season for me.

Thoughtful gesture. A few days before my husband left on a business trip, I sent him an "I miss you card." It was there when he arrived. He quickly phoned to thank me. Two days later, he received another. The next day, another. Each time he was pleasantly surprised. When he arrived home, there was even one on his pillow. While he was away, it made him smile and kept him thinking of me with fondness and a longing to come home.

Back in time. During a weekend trip to Bill's thirty year prep school reunion, we visited the Loretto Mother House, a place he had spent countless hours with his aunt who was then the Mother Superior. The nuns tutored him, did his laundry on weekends and prepared his meals. After hearing these stories for more than twenty years, visiting this place with him brought all those stories to life and held a very special meaning for me. If you have the chance, go with your spouse to places that hold fond memories. As with me, they will probably allow you a close-up glimpse of an early part of his life.

Give someone a gift. Make it a "no-special-occasion" present to your love or a good friend. Who knows? Romance can happen if you give your love a present and it's not even his birthday or hers. You'll be giving yourself some pleasure as well.

Speaking of gifts, there are many special occasions that call for them. They naturally show our affection and our appreciation to those we love and admire, but they must be chosen with thought and care.

Put as much into wrapping the gift as you do in choosing it. There is a myriad of paper and colors, including designer choices. There are printed decorative bags and marbleized boxes. Watch the professional gift wrappers, how they crease every seam. Let your package look as special.

Use a pretty ribbon, the wider the better, and tie a generous bow. Be creative. Make your own. Create several loops, tie in the middle and fluff out. For an extra touch, add a silk flower to your bow.

I once received a gift that was so wonderfully packaged, it took me ages to open it because I wanted to savor the beauty and the creativity of the wrap. My friend, Terry, put special effort into wrapping this gift. It definitely said, "I care!"

Use your creativity when giving. When I was in my twenties, it was the thing to give pantry showers for an engaged couple. Close to the wedding date we would hold a shower for the *couple* instead of merely the bride-to-be. We practically outfitted their kitchen and sometimes their bathroom cupboards giving them such things as spices, canned goods, cooking utensils, hot pads, potholders, dishtowels, paper towels, napkins, dishwashing detergent, sponges, scouring powders, pails, window cleaners, yard tools and anything non-perishable in the way of food items. For the bathroom: Shampoo, backbrush, bandaids, wastebasket, toothpaste, toothbrushes, lotions, bubblebath, tissues, hand soap and anything else pertinent to that room.

Whenever friends would buy a new house, there would usually be a surprise housewarming party, with everyone bringing a dish to pass and some chip-in money for a large gift such as a grill or a small electrical appliance. These showers were fun, yet practical.

Understanding. Everyone has their own struggles.

Try to understand why people do and say the things they do. You may never know of the crises or tragedies in their life to make them act as they do.

Be tolerant of the idiosyncracies of others. We all have them.

Respect your man. Treat him gently. Be conscious of the attention you give your love relationship. Don't ever take it for granted. Men: Let the one close to your heart know how special she is to you. Tell her often.

My husband has always allowed me to be "me". He has never tried to remake me or have me change my personality or ways of doing things. Keep this in mind as you might want to remold your partner to fit your image. It doesn't work.

Money definitely matters. Naturally, it doesn't buy love or happiness or a host of sound values. But without it, there is a decided lack of security and freedom. If you are lucky enough to have it, respect it and share it with countless others. You'll be enhancing your own life if you do. If you have it, don't put so much away for a rainy day that you can't enjoy it. With it, there comes a certain responsibility to not only share it with others, but also for yourself and your family to enjoy.

I have a friend who says, "I don't have much, but what I have, I share." And he does. He shares his two bedroom condo with those who have no place to go. If you have little, share it. If you have lots, share it.

My Mother, Josephine Monestero, believes and has often demonstrated what her Mother, Angelina Gerace, would say, "A house is as big as its owner wants it to be. No matter how small or how few beds or how little food on the table, there is always room enough for one more."

Make time. If someone asks you for a recipe and if you'd like to make the time (notice I did not say, 'if you *have* the time') prepare the item and hand deliver it along with the recipe.

Remind yourself there is always enough time for the important things. Think about the things you *make* time to do. These are what we want to do so we generally *find* the time. Think about the things you say you *don't have time for.* They are usually things you would rather not be doing. If it's important or if you want to, you will usually *find* the time to do it.

Visit your friends, but as my own parents would remind me, don't outwear your welcome. My father-in-law put it like this: "Go seldom where you know you're wanted and not at all when in doubt."

Thank you notes. One of the most fundamental rules of good manners. Stories abound from people who send gifts and receive no response. Every person who gives a gift, no matter what its value, is entitled to the courtesy of a thank you. A thank you is also in order after any gathering to which you have been invited. Get in the habit of sending thank you notes. Teach your children to send them.

If children are not reminded, the task gets forgotten. So I've tried setting the notes and the envelopes on my kitchen counter after my children have received gifts. They take the note and write it within a few days. The envelopes remain in my sight to remind me to in turn remind them until the deed is done.

When children are young, it is the parents' responsibility to see that this small task gets accomplished. Most children wouldn't take the initiative to do it on their own. Sometimes even older children need to be reminded.

> The two most important facets of writing thank you notes: • that they be straight from the heart • that they be sent immediately.

I know someone whose handwriting is letter perfect and exquisitely done. The first time I received something in the mail from her, I was in awe at the beauty of the handwriting. It nearly looked machine done. She confided to me once that she doesn't send many notes because it is very time consuming and she only wants them to go out if they look beautiful.

Don't be inclined to use your disdain of letter writing as an excuse not to send a note. Even a minimum effort is far better than none at all.

Crane's and Company, the popular stationery firm,

states it like this: "A Thank you which is poorly expressed or worse, not expressed at all - (after three days, you're late) exposes the erstwhile thanker as a boor. Just as the commercial thank you card will say to your benefactor, *I was too busy to thank you for your kindness.* Best not to be too busy or too late to thank someone for being kind to you.

If you keep a ready supply of paper and pens in a handy spot, you've already accomplished half of your task. Now, all you have to do is position yourself in this spot...and start. How do you do it? Here's a simple formula to follow:

---

1. Mention specifically why you are saying thank you:
Dear Joan:
Thank you for the lovely address and date book for my graduation.
2. Tell them exactly what it is you like about it and what you plan to do with it:
Now I have my own place to record all of my personal information about my friends. It will help to keep me organized and help me to remember birthdays and other special days.
3. Mention when you might see your giftgiver:
I hope to see you soon. Love Kathy.

Just mention it, what you will do with it, and sign your name. This method is short, yet personal.

Whistling is very uplifting and it's an incredible workout for the lungs, says a 39 year-old national whistling champion from Horsham, Pennsylvania. "It makes me happy and it makes others happy, too." She says she does warbles, trills, and pursed-lip breathing and shows others how too. Whistling helps people with lung problems breathe easier as it expands their lungs. Did you know that there is a National Whistlers' Convention? I remember my mother whistling often when I was growing up. So if you want to make some music, give a little whistle!

Graciousness. How many times have you asked, "How are you?" and received a "ho-hum" response: "Ohhh, alll riiight!" or "Not tooo bad", or "Just so-so", in a whining tone to go with the negative words?

NO WHINING !

Even if you don't feel it, the next time someone asks how you are, say: "Great" or "I'm very well, thank you and you?" or "Fine, thank you, how are you?"

We must train our children in this vein. My Greek friend, Michael, asked my daughter who was nine at the time, "How are you?" Her response: "Fine." Period. Michael looked at me and said, "Every kid in America, when asked how they are, says fine and nothing more." He was right. My grandparents were Italian immigrants. They brought with them the gracious greeting and response: *Fine, thank you, and how are you?* I always heard my parents use it, as well.

How are you is a part of hello. It's a greeting, not

an inquiry about your physical or mental status. One person I knew years ago mimicked, when I said Hello, how are you? *"That's all everyone says is 'hi, how are you, hi, how are you?' Can't anyone just say hi?"* What was her objection in answering, *fine, thank you, and you?* How sad that she felt this way and how obnoxious that she voiced it. I never again asked how she was.

When someone inquires as to how you are, be gracious in your response. Continual answers like, "I could be better" and after a good morning from someone, "What's good about it?" usually come from shallow-thinking people. Where has graciousness gone?

When you think of being gracious, think of what the word actually means: friendly, polite, tender, mild, gentle, benevolent, courteous, compassionate. Though we may not practice these ways everyday in every interaction we have, at least striving for them is a step toward inner beauty.

You don't have to do great things to give joy. Do as Sister Teresa suggests: "...only small things with *great* love."

Importance. One popular author reminds us that we never have proof of our importance, but we are, indeed, more important than we know.

Someone told me once that she was feeling stressful in her job. She was in a position to cut back her hours which she immediately did. In doing so, she felt a burden lifted. She took care of her very important self. As she related this story to me, she said, "I learned to do that from you, Carol." What surprised me was that I wasn't aware of teaching any such thing. People watch and learn from us all the time, and we teach when we're least aware. Your importance is what others learn from your example. Let it be good.

—————

Who among us at times has not felt important? Indeed, it can be a weighty feeling. This feeling might have been created from within or triggered by someone else.

Wherever it comes from doesn't matter. The relevance is that it be there at all. We know what it feels like to glow. And if we practice the principle that has been around for eons, namely: "Do unto others as you would have them do unto you," then we would want others to glow as well. For if we help others to feel radiant and important, we automatically have those qualities returned to us like a boomerang.

Professor John Dewey has stated that the deepest urge in human nature is the desire to feel important and Professor William James said that the deepest principle in human nature is the craving to be appreciated.

Do you want to feel important? Or be appreciated? Do you want a little recognition for the person you are? For the things you do?

Then, look for something to admire in others, even when you think there may be nothing. Find a redeeming value or something you can say or do to make that person feel important and appreciated.

Start today and do it regularly. If your tone has

been other than appropriate, change it and speak to others in a complimentary fashion whenever you can. Never falsely, but speak warm words of affection and show the magic of appreciation in a true, sincere and genuine manner.

If you admire someone, don't keep it a secret. Tell them. Even if you have to write them a letter, do it. Most people feel they are important. Very important. But it is sweet music, indeed, when someone else affirms it. So work the magic now. Don't you be the only one to feel important. Let others feel it too.

Affirmations. Phil Barnhart, Pastor of the Chapel on the Hill Church in Lake Geneva, Wisconsin, puts out a monthly newsletter. Every newsletter has pertinent information in it. I look forward to these mini sermons because they're almost always something to which I can relate, and they almost always put a smile on my face.

One day I jotted a note to Phil to tell him what a great job I thought he was doing, how much his newsletters meant to me and how much I enjoyed his writing.

This busy man took the time to answer my note. It seems he was grateful for my comments. They meant a lot to him. He thanked me for the affirmation.

Months later, I received a booklet he had written on how to live life to the fullest and how to get more out of it. In it he talks about the fact that much of our lives is the sum total of contributions from other people. It is his contention that we should give more testimonials on behalf of those who have enriched our lives.

When you consider the contributions you have made, most likely it is because of the positive influence of other people. If you'd like to give credit to those who have made a mark on you, here's how: Think about these people. Who are they and what did they contribute to your life? Was it your parents, teachers, friends, counselors, former employers, pastors, church members? The list could probably go on and on.

Once you know who these people are, recall what they have done to add to your life. Next, sit down and communicate your appreciation to those people. After many years, Phil had written to one of his high school teachers to let her know how she had influenced his life. Her reply was that in forty years of teaching, his letter was the first such correspondence she had ever received.

Lack of communication is one of the many reasons today for relationships going amuck. If you appreciate someone, let them know. Tell them.

The following poem expresses it nicely:

I would rather have one little rose
From the garden of a friend
Than have the choicest flowers
When my day on earth must end.
I would rather have a pleasant word
In kindness said to me
Than flattery when my heart is still,
When life has ceased to be.
I would rather have a loving smile
From friends I know are true.
Than tears shed at my casket

Carol Fitzgerald

When the world I bid adieu.
Bring me all your flowers today
Whether pink or white or red
I'd rather have one blossom now
Than a truckload when I'm dead.

(author unknown)

If someone has been kind to you or added immeasurably to your life, let them know how grateful you are. Do it today.

Give joy. One of my biggest treasures as a child was a new box of crayons. I colored incessantly and my crayons wore down often. I liked fresh new points and every time I got a brand new box of pointy crayons, I was on top of the world. Guess I wasn't the only one. Billions, yes billions, of these things a year are manufactured. If your child or you know a child who has a shoebox filled with stubs, give him or her a bit of joy and buy a new box of crayons or markers. I know a nun who teaches in South America. She has boxes and boxes of stubs for her little charges, and is grateful for every one.

Countless acts of thoughtlessness and unkindnesses happen everyday with nary an utterance of, "I'm sorry." Make an amend if you have offended someone. Tell them you're sorry. Attempt to bridge a gulf by saying, "Let's start over," or "What can I do to fix what I've undone?" Sometimes just a change in perspective can set you on a new course with your estranged person.

19

If you've sincerely tried all you can and are still not able to win the party to your side or repair any damages, then drop it. You've tried. They are not accepting your attempts at reconciliation. Then it becomes their problem. Let it go and go on!

On the other hand, do *you* need to forgive someone? Do it now. Someone to forgive could also be yourself. Don't beat yourself up for long or carry on unnecessary guilt. Whatever has happened is past history. You need to do whatever you can to make an amend to yourself or others, then get on with your life and don't let it occupy your mind another minute.

Let Go Of Guilt

A major faux pas. Once an invitation for Sunday night "snacks" did not get marked on our calendar. One hour after we should have been there, we received a telephone call wondering where we were. Horrified that we had committed such a major faux pas, we quickly dressed and made a bee-line to our destination. We arrived out of breath, angry at ourselves and fully embarrassed, apologing with every step into the house. When we saw that the table was fully set, we knew clearly that we had been invited for more than "snacks." And to top it off, we had already had our meal. Neither of us was hungry, but there was no way we could add insult to injury after having been so late. We ate another meal. The evening turned out to be thoroughly delightful, interesting and informative.

But the next day, I was still feeling more than a bit

guilty. Things like this don't usually happen because I'm one of those notorious types. I write almost everything down. I'm one of those proverbial list-makers. How could I have let such a kind invitation slip by unnoticed? I promptly wrote a note and went to the florist to choose a colorful bouquet. Bill hand-delivered the flowers. Later I talked with the hostess who, incidentally, handled the entire affair with the utmost graciousness. She never questioned or even remarked about our being late. She welcomed us in with the smile and warmth of an angel as though we'd arrived on time. Now here was a woman of beauty: gracious and accommodating in every way never letting us feel anything but glad to be there. Wow! Was I impressed and did I ever learn a lesson!!

Anyway, she told me that Bill arriving with the flowers was a bright spot in her day. She nurtured, sung to and talked to those flowers and she said they lasted for several days.

These things can happen to anyone. But ignoring a situation, if it does happen, is where the insult in heaped upon the injury. Just make an apology if one is needed. Just do it. Here are some ways: Send flowers or deliver your own as we did. Tuck in a note. Make a phone call. Write a letter. Send a gift. Take over a cake or some cookies.

If you say you are too busy to do any of that, then you are not living. You are merely existing. In fact, John H. Rhoades sums it up this way:

Do more than exist, live
Do more than touch, feel

Do more than look, observe
Do more than read, absorb
Do more than hear, listen
Do more than listen, understand
Do more than think, ponder
Do more than talk, say something

Being the right person. I know a man. A very gentle man. He treats everyone he encounters, loved ones and strangers alike, in a kind and gentle manner. He knows not the meaning of a harsh word to others. He does not criticize, nor does he judge.

At times when he is criticized, he merely accepts. He does not deny, nor does he argue or justify. When he is judged, he does not let it weigh heavily on his soul. Nor does he take it personally. Instead, he tries to understand the reasons for people's words and actions. To put it simply, he lives and lets live.

His philosophy mirrors that of Henry James:

> "The first thing to learn in intercourse with others is noninterference with their own peculiar ways of being happy..."

This man interferes with no one, not even those closest to him. In order to get his point across, he does so with a sense of humor.

I especially like the way he treats his wife. No matter what she says or does, he never reproaches her in public or in private. He accepts her for who she is and allows her to be her own self, not one he would have her be.

Consider this. If his wife needs support, he gives it to her. If she needs encouragement, he gives that to her. He still presents her with an occasional bouquet of flowers. He offers her money freely and never questions how or where she spends it. He makes an effort to understand her periods of moodiness and irritability. He grasps many opportunities to praise her. He admires her and never hesitates to tell her that she is a good wife and a wonderful mother. He often tells her how nice she looks or how good she smells. He even remembers to thank her for the little things she does for him.

After more than twenty-five years of marriage, he still drives her to the door of a restaurant or public building, *then* he parks the car. He treats her with the tenderness one would a precious newborn baby.

As Leland Foster Wood wrote in his book, *Growing Together in the Family,* "Success in marriage is much more than a matter of *finding* the right person; it is also a matter of *being* the right person."

This man definitely knows how to *be* the right person.

Along the same lines, Disraeli's wife was a master at this very art in their wonderfully successful marriage. She was a rich widow when he married her for her money and freely admitted he did not and would not marry for love.

She did not have such things going for her as youth, beauty and intelligence, nor even style in clothing or furnishings. She often erred in her literary and histori-

23

cal conversations. What, then, made their marriage so successful? She knew one thing well. And that was how to handle her man:

She adored her husband and praised him often. She helped and advised him whenever she could. She was also his friend and his confidante. Perhaps one of her most endearing qualities was that she believed he could achieve and be successful at whatever he attempted. She let him know that her faith in him was paramount and that he simply could not fail.

She did not nag, nor did she criticize or complain about the way he looked or the things he did wrong. She was not jealous. She did not scold. In short, she cherished him.

It has been said that, "Many a wife has made her own marital grave with a series of little digs." On the contrary, Mary Anne paid little attentions toward Disraeli: small, everyday attentions which were the foundation and the support for their marriage. If I were to guess at what her thoughtfulness consisted of, I would say they might include: saying please and thank you, giving a backrub now and then, turning down his side of the bed covers, leaving notes in inconspicuous places, looking him in the eye and smiling, telling him she believed in and supported him, asking *him* out on a date, telling him she loved him, telling him she liked him and in general letting him know she cared.

One of Edna St. Vincent Millay's rhymes says it succinctly:

> "Tis not love's going hurts my days,
> But that it went in little ways."

To have that quality of heart that overlooks the weeds and sees the flowers in the garden instead, this would probably be a start toward paying little courtesies.

Disraeli would tease Mary Anne and say, "You know, I only married you for your money, anyhow." And Mary Anne would answer with a smile, "Yes, but if you had it to do over again, you would marry me for love, wouldn't you?"

And he said that was true.

Mary Anne knew the value of courtesy in dealing with this man who only married her for her money. And in the end this thing called courtesy played a major role in his ultimate feelings for her.

Arguing. Have you ever heard these words?
"You're wrong."
"No!"
"It's not that way at all."
"Can't you see it my way?"
"I'll prove it to you."
Do they sound familiar? If so, read on:

You may be able to prove your argument, but why would you want to prove a person wrong? Why would you want to create an uncomfortable atmosphere by continually telling the other person he or she is wrong and you are right?

Usually the more we argue, the less headway we make. The more we push our point of view, the less

25

apt the other person is to see it. Consider this:

> "A man convinced against his will is of the same opinion still."

Minds are not changed by arguments. In fact, the person who loses the argument generally goes away feeling a bit inferior, probably has had his or her pride hurt, and most likely holds some negative feelings toward the person who said he or she was wrong.

> Benjamin Franklin said this: "If you argue and rankle and contradict, you may achieve a victory sometimes; but it will be an empty victory because you will never get your opponent's good will."

People want to feel important. Telling them they are wrong sends the message they are unimportant.

Now, people change their minds everyday; but if someone tries to change it for them, they cling fast to their beliefs and ideas. So it seems that it is not really the ideas we don't want changed, it is the mere fact that we are being told to change them.

Those who are honest might admit their wrongs to themselves. And if someone gently tries to persuade, we might give in to them. But probably never will we admit a wrong if someone smugly reminds us of it. For, "men must be taught as if you taught them not, and things unknown proposed as things forgot." If you want to prove your point, do it so that no one will ever be aware of it happening.

Stuff happens as the phrase sometimes goes...to everyone. The big secret is knowing that we all have the capacity to adjust.

Be there for your friends. Make friends with people who want to be there for you.

In Barbara Bush's speech to new graduates of Pueblo Community College, she said, "Never lose sight of the fact that the most important yardstick of your success will be how you treat other people, your family, friends and co-workers and even strangers you meet along the way." She went on to say, "Being a parent, a daughter, a son, a sister, a brother or somebody's best friend is the most important role you play in this life."

I read something once that went like this: There are two kinds of people in the world: Those who walk into a room and say, *There you are* and those who say, *Here I am.* Which category are you in?

Kindness. A few basic concepts my Mother taught me seem to have perched in the forefront of my mind: "Be considerate, kind, and thoughtful," she would often say. These concepts formed and remain today, the very basis of etiquette. But first be kind to yourself. Being kind to others will then follow.

Don't say, 'Let's get together' more than once. Either set a date and issue an invitation or say nothing.

Research a family tree and preserve your family

history for future generations. There are professional genealogists located throughout the country to help you in your search for family members. There are also database services who help with research and can provide information about names that are given to them.

Gifts. Keep a gift drawer. Buy things when you see them that you think might make good gifts. When you need a gift in a hurry, precious time will be saved by not having to run out and buy one. You will already have a selection from which to choose. Things like book plates, magnetic list pads, small books, book marks, stationery, pretty napkins or coasters, candles, bath salts, lotion, picture frames, small photo albums. Things like that.

Many women I know really seem to have a sixth sense...perhaps otherwise known as intuition? Men: Trust it! Susan Branch in her book *Love from the Heart of the Home* quotes Edward Dahlberg on Women:

"A Woman is the most superstitious animal beneath the moon. When a woman has a premonition that Tuesday will be a disaster, to which a man pays no heed, he will very likely lose his fortune then. This is not meant to be an occult or mystic remark. The female body is a vessel, and the universe drops its secrets into her far more quickly than it communicates them to the male."* Men: Take heart!

* *Used by permission from Little Brown and Company*

Share your talents. Do you play a musical instrument? Entertain those who don't. Do you sing? Join a choir or choral group. Share your special talent for others to enjoy or better yet, teach them.

Sense of humor. If you have a sense of humor, use it. Make others laugh. This is a rare gift and not everyone has this wonderful ability. When our daughter, Keri, was younger, she once said to me in a rather exasperated tone, "Oh, Mom. You laugh at everything Dad says." As a young adult woman, she now has me laughing at many of the things she says. She seems to have inherited this splendid trait from her father. She can retell a story with uncanny wit. She keeps her family laughing as she does those around her at her workplace. Even though this seems to be a gift, I think it can be cultivated. Be aware of the funny stuff that happens around you. Then relate that to others.

Flowers are fantastic! What is it about them that can send a spirit soaring or brighten a room or change your outlook? They are an important part of living. They're colorful. They make bold statements. They're both impressive and expressive, and the fragrance of some can pack a powerful punch.

Every so often I will pluck a gardenia or two and set them around the house in shallow containers. One very special place is

29

on my bedside table so that throughout the night I can catch hints of their glorious fragrance.

When I lived in Chicago, I had neighbors who nurtured gardenias in their greenhouse. They knew my weakness and every now and then, in the cold of winter, would cradle a gardenia in cupped hands and walk it down the block to me.

Fresh flowers are usually sent only on special occasions, and many people will only order for themselves when they are giving a party. How sweet to have fresh flowers surround us everyday. Gladiolus in the supermarket beckon to me every time I pass by them. They usually win. I can't ignore their call - I grab a bunch or even two. And once they're arranged, I revel in their stately beauty for nearly a week. They never fail to put a smile on my face and joy in my heart.

Even though they don't last long, I still like to have their beauty surround me. But they can be costly. If this is a problem, perhaps you can budget for them. Sacrifice something else for the week and buy flowers, instead. Or although not fresh, do what I did the other day. I bought one dusty colored silk rose for sixty-nine cents, put it in a clear vase with water (the water gives the initial impression that it is fresh) and set it on my bathroom counter. Joy! It gives me pure joy every time I walk in there and see it. So indulge yourself. Part with a few cents and put a silk flower in a vase with water.

All of this talk about flowers and I must make mention of consideration for those who are allergic. Please be aware of those whom flowers negatively affect.

Though the scents can be lovely to most, they can trigger some nasty reactions in others. If you fall into this category, silks might be your choice, instead.

There are also those who enjoy and take much pleasure in arranging their own flowers. Yet, there are others who are all thumbs and would rather leave this task to the florists. In any event, change the water regularly in your arrangements. As the flowers start to fade and wilt, instead of pitching the whole bouquet, trim what is no longer pretty and rearrange the still-perky stems into smaller vases.

Vases, too, can add to the impact of your arrangement. Generally, a vase should be smaller than the spread of the flowers. Sometimes the stems can be arranged in a pinwheel swirl, so that in a see-through vase they can be an impressive sight. A vase that is too large can dwarf the flowers. If it is wrong in any way, it can make them appear skimpy or rigid. If one vase doesn't work, try another.

I have a collection of vases I have gathered over the years with trips to antique shops. Invariably when I arrange flowers, the first one never seems to be right. So, I just go through my collection until I find the perfect size. Whatever your feelings about flowers, keep these tips in mind when you give flowers as a gift:

Twelve flowers remind the Germans of our phrase, "Cheaper by the dozen." Also in Germany, only sweethearts send each other roses. So if you're sweet on someone, send red roses to get your message across.

Red roses in France are a symbol of the

31

Socialist party and are not a welcome gift. White lilies in Great Britain are reserved for funerals.

While Keri was still in college, she sent to me a single, solitary, coral hued rose. This created more of an impact on me than a dozen or more would have.

Flowers are truly uplifting to the spirit. If you want to lift your own, buy a bunch and arrange them throughout your house. If you want to lift the spirits of another, send a bouquet. Or even one stem will do. Better yet, deliver them in person.

What man doesn't like flowers? Give yours a flower or two, or even a bunch.

Wondering what to give the man with no hobbies? Buy an azalea plant or a rose bush or a flowering tree. My Dad has nurtured his such gifts with tender loving care.

The calling card used centuries ago, is thought to have originated in China. The custom of "leaving a card" began in Italy during the 16th century. France later adopted the custom and from there it spread to Great Britain.

The original purpose of the calling or visiting card was to hand to a servant when calling on someone who was not at home. These cards were bedecked with flowers, borders, scrolls and other designs. Early in the 19th century, the name, engraved on a fine card stock, was the only embellishment; all other designs discontinued.

Naturally, since formal calls are rarely made in these

days of swift living, formal calling cards are also rarely used. The custom does remain in the world of the military, governmental and diplomatic circles and in some areas of the United States and in European and Eastern countries.

Despite the fact that the original use of the calling card has diminished, there are many social ways it can be used today: enclosed with gifts or flowers for short messages, for issuing or replying to invitations and for introducing yourself.

There are times when you might want to exchange your name and phone number with someone you've just met. Rather than tearing the corner of your deposit slip from your checkbook or searching for a piece of scratch paper in your purse, a more graceful, social gesture would be to present a card with your name engraved or printed on it, instead. These are available at your local printer or through mail order houses.

Carol Fitzgerald

(Address & Phone Optional)

If you use your card as a flower gift enclosure, you may want to include a brief message. If you are sending a gift from the store, write the person's name on the matching envelope but not the address. Seal it only if you have written a personal message. No message should be written on a wedding gift card enclosure as the card is generally displayed along with the gift.

The use of fragrance is an important aspect in the "finishing" of your total self. As our choice of clothing reveals a bit about us overall, so too does the scent we choose to waft about us.

Do you only wear perfume when you go out? If you enjoy scents, and you or those around you are not allergic, wear it everyday. Even when you know you are going nowhere, make it a point to lather yourself in perfumed lotion or spray on your favorite scent for your own sensory enjoyment. Even wear perfume or lotion to bed. Vary the scent you wear. After awhile, you will no longer be able to smell it on yourself.

An important note to consider when selecting a perfume is that the fragrances change as they mix with your own unique skin chemistry. So, try the free samples that are given in department stores, and experiment until you find the right one for you. Or, the strips that come in magazines or in your monthly statements. Fragrance experts also say that dark complexions hold fragrances differently than fair-complexioned skins. In addition, there is a "dry-down" effect, about a "10 minute period for the true scent to develop."

A cover-up, perfume is not; although in the very early ages, this is precisely what it was. Fragrances, extracts and scented balms were used abundantly to take the place of a lack of bathing facilities. In fact, one of the kings in the French Renaissance was known as "the sweetest smelling monarch". Napoleon supposedly used sixty bottles of cologne a month.

The role of perfume has changed from cover-up to pleasing sensory perceptions. The Middle Ages saw the use of perfume develop into a full-fledged industry, with France at the center creating delicious scents.

Perfume manufacturing takes place in the world capital of Grasse, a rural area in the south of France. Here, there is an ever abundant profusion of glorious color and fragrance in the incessantly blooming flower beds. The flowers of Grasse are grown especially for making perfume. The beds and fields of the array of flowers are preserved at night by being packed in straw. When ready, the flowers are gingerly hand-picked and scurried to the factory, where the fragrance is drawn from the blossoms.

The basic classes of perfumes are single floral, floral bouquet, spicy, citrus, Oriental, green, woodsy-mossy, and fruity.

Again, it may take some trial testing to determine to which class your skin best reacts. Consider the following variations:

- *Perfume - the most concentrated and the longest lasting; also the most expensive.*
- *Perfume water - not as strong or as expensive; lasts from two to five hours.*
- *Toilet water - lighter and more subtle; evaporates quickly; lasts two to four hours.*
- *Cologne - lightest scent; can be synthetic; is the most popular form in America and lasts one to three hours.*

• *Cream perfume concentrate - solid cream-based scent; best suited to dry skin. Longer lasting.*

Perfumes can be magical, and we react both physically and emotionally to their fragrances. Perfumes can also be overdone. As you splash on your scents, be careful not to go overboard. All you need is a subtle hint. Find the scent that's right for you and, as a television ad would say, make a statement...without saying a word! But again, do remember those who are sensitive to scents.

Do yourself a favor. There are some days when nothing can go wrong. You wonder what you've done to deserve all the good that's happening in your life. Then, there are those days when nothing seems right. At every turn, you run into a brick wall. These are times that have you wishing morning wouldn't come and you didn't have to go to work today. Sometimes major changes need to be made; other times, only minor steps need to be taken.

Whatever the case, you do have the right, as the saying goes, "to be good to yourself." After all, if we continually beat ourselves, running, going, shopping, doing, working, cooking, and more, then every bit of energy has been used and we're sufficiently drained. Contrary to what Tennessee Ernie Ford sang in the song, "Sixteen Tons", you *don't* owe your soul to the company store, whether it's at home or at the office. It's time to ask, "What can I do to feel good again?"

Is it a massage? Then book an appointment for

one. Join a health club? Do it. Visit a spa? Go! A manicure? Get one. If you think about your body...and your mind...as the engine that pulls the load, keeping them in tiptop shape would probably be a major priority. If they are in tiptop condition, then life isn't such a heavy burden.

Are you shackled to your desk? To your home? To your work in whatever form it takes? Loosen the chains you've put around yourself and take an hour or two, if you can't manage a day or two. Take long weekends, if you can't manage a week or more. Stroll on your lunch hour. Pack a lunch and eat it in the park, on a lake or at the beach. This is therapy at its finest and it doesn't cost anything. Some would also call shopping therapy, but that's a bit more expensive.

Get involved in sports if you are a sports enthusiast. When you go to bed at night tired, at least you will have the full confidence of knowing you are tired from doing something you enjoyed. Do the things that make you comfortable. Join the airline clubs if you travel a lot. Instead of chomping at the bit when flights are delayed, wait in the comfort of the rooms these clubs offer. Conduct meetings at the airport instead of shuttling to hotels. Or, when you are in a hotel, take advantage of room service.

Finally, nothing in business is so important that you lose sight of the person who matters most to you. Plan a romantic dinner.

Is there a life hidden here somewhere beyond work and all? You bet. Suddenly, that "bah humbug" attitude and the gruff voice and the harsh answers that were becoming a part of you are no longer there. Do yourself a favor and make your life a little easier.

Ring a bell to announce that dinner is ready instead of calling or yelling. No, not just for guests, but for your children too.

A box idea. Have your children fill shoe boxes at Christmas time for the homeless adults, or for disadvantaged children and teenagers. Wrap the tops and bottoms of the boxes separately so they will have something visually appealing in which to store their items. After the box has been filled and the wrapped top in place, tie with a lovely bow. Items to use: playing cards, chewing gum, toothpaste, toothbrush, lotion, combs, shampoo, bar soap, candy bars, dried soup, pencils, pens, scotch tape, crayons, paper clips, coloring books, nail polish, a paperback book, postcards and/or postage stamps, gift certificates for a hamburger and a coke or tickets to a movie theater.

Book thoughts. Include a blank book plate when you give a book as a gift. Write some meaningful words on the inside cover. One of my favorites when giving children's books is a quote by Strickland Gillian:

> "Emeralds and Rubies and Riches untold.
> Caskets of Silver, coffers of gold.
> Richer than I you can never be.
> I had a mother who read to me."

Another is by Charles Lamb who said, "Lose yourself in other men's minds."

I jot notes many times as an automatic gesture, but one time I gave a book forgetting to write anything. Bill's cousin told me that the first thing she did when I gave them books as gifts was to look on the inside cover for my note. When she found none  this particular time, she was disappointed. I hadn't realized how important this gesture was at least to one person.

Learn a new skill. Typing, bridge, a foreign language, dancing, sewing, scuba diving. Take a computer course. Anything to help add some pizzazz to your life...and some self-confidence perchance?

Make a new friend; someone you admire perhaps. Call and set a date for coffee or lunch. Ask a new couple you've met to join you and your love for a hamburger. Maybe a friendship will form. Maybe not.

Use color. I was at a school volunteer meeting one morning with all of my information in a pink file folder. The pink caught the attention of the woman sitting next to me. She smiled and commented on it. Would a manilla one have evoked the same smile and comment?

At ease. Try to put everyone you meet at ease. Introduce yourself to someone new in a gathering. Smile if you can't think of anything to say. It's usually a beginning. Questions, the open-ended kind, are great for conversation. Stay away from questions that can only be answered by yes or no. I call them monosyllabic: one word answers. Kind of leaves you just standing there, searching for another question. Some people call them door slammers. They slam the door on further conversation. Think about beginning questions with who, what, when, where, and how. Here are a few open-ended ones for starters: How does a rainy day make you feel? What is your favorite thing to do on a rainy day? Are you ambitious or do you procrastinate? What are some of your pet peeves? What are some things that make you angry? Happy? Questions like these can be used in groups, with your love and even your children. They can probably spur others to think and keep you both in conversation for awhile.

A nice gesture. Coming home on Sunday evenings from weekend trips tired and with small children in tow, many times, we found a dozen eggs, a gallon of milk and a loaf of bread at our door by a friend and former neighbor. This was always such a treat. Tired, we were spared a stop at the grocery store. What a beautiful, thoughtful gesture from one who was helpful in every way. We all know people like this, always willing to lend a hand. They're the type to brighten the lives of others.

Another nice gesture. A tired and hungry honeymoon couple had an inventive and creative mother. She had prepared for them, upon their return, a basket filled with gourmet goodies for their first dinner at home: Cheese, bread, fresh fruit, dessert, champagne and even some candles and fresh flowers.

Are you new in town, feeling a bit disjointed and not as secure as you would like? Are your friends and family a distance away and you feel lonely? Do you and your children need some new friends? Are you newly single and want to form fresh associations? Perk up. These feelings won't last long if you are open to change and some new ideas and suggestions. Though not original, a friend of mine reiterated the other day, "Fifty per cent of life is showing up." Nothing will change, of course, if you sit back and wait for it to happen. So if you can conjure up some energy and time, get ready and willing, and be receptive and perceptive, *and show up*, you will be on the road to meeting people and making new friends.

You'll naturally want to do this with as much ease as possible; you'll need to gear up for it. If you want to meet people, you'll have to be meetable yourself.

Think back on the times you've met others. Which meetings stand out in your mind? Those where the person stepped forward with hand extended and greeted you with a friendly sincerity? Or was it the self confident aura the person exuded? Maybe it was the body language, standing comfortably erect, or leaning forward in conversation? Most certainly this person you remember must have had a warm smile and a genuine approach. Or was it someone with a sense of humor?

"The only thing we have to fear is fear itself." - Franklin Delano Roosevelt

If you hold back in fear, you will be assuming a passive role. Someone once said, "Passivity makes you very quickly forgettable." If forgettable is not what you want to be, then be the one to step forward (not aggressively, just assertively). Easier said than done, you say? Well, hone your meeting skills by talking to people wherever you go: waiting in lines, in doctors' offices or on elevators. Just a little small talk. Most people are friendly and will respond in kind. If they don't no harm done. Don't persist if you feel it would be a bother to them. But you won't know unless you try; it's good practice.

Insecure people will many times look everywhere but directly at the people they are talking to or meeting. A wall is suddenly erected which shields and protects them. Sometimes these walls can be penetrated and sometimes they cannot. If you encounter such people and with your charm cannot break their barrier, so be it. The important thing to remember, if you are uncomfortable when meeting people, is not to build defenses around yourself. Enjoy the challenge, rather than fight it.

In order to make meeting people a positive force in your life, put on a happy face, even if you don't feel like it. I repeat, Smile. Stick only with positive remarks and never complain about anything. If you are feeling down and not quite tip top, don't let on. Find something about which you can be cheerful and then communicate that.

Not only is it a good idea to say something pleasant, but it is also important to be pleasant to everyone you meet, even to those who may not be so pleasant to you or even to those who are cranky. Remember: "A soft answer turneth away wrath." Try it and watch the calm come over a disgruntled customer or service employee.

Take the initiative, even if you have to force yourself. If you practice these principles often enough, soon they will become habit and you will discover that meeting people is not so bad after all.

GET INVOLVED
Ways To Meet New People:
• Classes. There is an abundance of adult education classes where you could focus an interest and perhaps meet others who share that interest.

• If your forté is athletic, join a team or go at it individually. Even if you are not good at sports, try this pastime anyway. It's a great way to meet people.

• Beach activities. Organize picnics, volleyball games, contests of one sort or another.

• Boating or Sailing. Take a course in sailing or join a yacht club. These are good groups with which to associate and fun seems to be their main objective.

• Entertaining. Accept all party invitations, business or social. Give some parties yourself, even if you don't know many people to invite. One way to get acquainted in a new area is to invite two couples to your party. In turn, have each of them invite two couples or two sets of singles, and the second two couples invite two more couples. At least two couples will know the four people they have invited, but no one will know everyone. Have each couple bring a dish to pass and voila, an instant reservoir of new acquaintances. As an icebreaker, play some games.

• Children's activities. If you volunteer and get involved in what your children do, you are bound to meet the parents of your children's friends. You could always invite several parents of your child's friends for a potluck and include the children in the plans.

• Gourmet groups. If cooking is your specialty, you might find one of these clubs a pleasant way to meet others and expand your culinary expertise at the same time. It wouldn't even have to be gourmet. Candlelight Dinner is what my group is called. It centers around food. There are anywhere from thirty to forty people in the large group but only four couples meet together at various homes throughout the year. There are different groups of eight at each dinner and everyone takes a turn at being host and hostess with the other couples sharing the rest of the courses in the meal. The large group meets together once a year. The smaller groups are a good opportunity for people to get to know each other better. (See p. 154 for the rotating diagram).

• Newspaper. Tune in to the People Briefs or Things To Do section in your daily paper. Local happenings are listed here.

• Shopping. Strike up conversations with people as you shop or wait in lines at the grocery store.

• Support Groups. Wonderful fellowships are formed in the many programs which help to support various medical and other problems. There are Alcoholics Anonymous, Al-Anon and Alateen, Overeaters Anonymous, Gamblers Anonymous, Narcotics Anonymous, Families Anonymous, Workaholics Anonymous, Parents Without Partners, Singles groups and a myriad of others. Call the national associations for more information.

Nearly every one of the major diseases has a support group and the national organization can offer information for local chapters.

• Single...widowed...divorced? Dust off your dancing shoes and gear up for fun! There are dance cruises for those ages 50 - 90, beginners or advanced, who love to dance but who don't have a partner. Expert and charming gentlemen hosts are aboard to dine with, then whirl you around the dance floor. Sponsored by the Triple AAA Auto Club South, the Merry Widow Dance Cruises and Tours offer sun-filled days and fun-filled nights. Call them at 1-800-374-2689 or write Phyllis Zeno, Director, AAA Merry Widows, Box 31087, Tampa, Florida 33631.

• Dances. Join a class, take lessons at the social dance studio or attend any of the dances you hear about. If ballroom dance is your style, do that. Line dancing or country dancing is fun too.

Whichever way you decide is right for you to meet people, do it. Research the various ways; get involved by volunteering, but do get involved. New people will not be knocking on your door. You must be the one to seek them out.

Praise, don't criticize. Tell a child, a spouse, a friend or an employee that he is dumb or stupid or can't do a particular thing, or that he doesn't know how, or he isn't doing it right, and you've just programmed him into believing it himself. Further, any incentive to do better has now been squelched. You have probably also scored a point against yourself. Perhaps a better technique would be to encourage the person instead. Let him see the ease in a situation or a task rather than point out the difficulty. Place your confidence in him and let him know he has the ability or that he might have a flair for it. Give him the gift of believing in himself. Say things like: "Good job," or "I have confidence that you will make the right decision," or "you're a great kid and I love you," or "I know you will work hard to do the very best you can."

If a person is made to feel he can do something, then his attempt at it would not be so formidable. He will go into a new situation, a new task, anything new, with a positive attitude and will more likely feel he will succeed.

Everyone has redeeming qualities and talents, but many times these very qualities are overshadowed by a person's obvious inabilities to perform in certain other situations.

It is during these times that you might automatically strike out by scolding or ridiculing, thereby hindering any possibility of development.

Hold your temper. Emphasizing one's mistakes and obvious errors discourages people. Praise, on the other hand, adds to their self-esteem.

Errors need to be minimized and right deeds maximized in order for a person to reach higher levels.

So, if you want to be an influencing factor in helping others to reach those higher levels, if you want to get along with people, if you want to instill hope and the desire to improve, don't criticize. Don't find fault. Build up, give confidence and dole out heaps of genuine encouragement and praise instead.

Notes and greetings. There is a place most of my family heads for as they walk in the door to our house. It is the central location where we write notes to one another...a place to communicate when no one is home. Basically, it's a place to find out, "Did anyone call?" and "Where are you?" But we also leave other notes there, too.

This message center is the life blood of our keeping in touch with each other, our communication on busy days when we're all running, and for things forgotten to be said when we're together.

"Where is everyone?" is a common query at our house, too, even if only one or two of us are not there. When we walk in and find no one there, we want to know. So, it has become a custom and a matter of courtesy for us to leave a note saying where we are and about when we will return.

This message-leaving trend has been a family affair for generations. My parents wrote notes to me. I left notes for them. I write my children and husband notes and they leave notes for me.

We have even left notes in unexpected places: coat or shirt pockets, lunch boxes, on the bathroom mirror, in the car, in books they are reading, on the inside of the front door, on their bed, right smack on the television screen and even in the refrigerator. We leave funny notes. We leave serious notes. And we leave plain, everyday, ordinary notes, all to say, "I am thinking of you," in various ways.

In addition to written messages, spoken greetings are also important. My parents greeted me with a "Good Morning" when I was a baby, and I learned to return the same greeting. We say, "Good Morning" in our house and in my classroom when I've taught.

At the end of the day we also say, "Goodnight." Merely to disappear with no greeting seems as if something is missing. It's a final note at the close of the day to say, "I'll see you in the morning."

⟫◦⟨

On the morning of Bill's 50th, I left him a birthday note. When I saw his pleasure in finding and reading it, I decided to write another note and another. And yet another. At every turn of his step, he ran into these notes on various colors of paper and cards with varied colored inks and designs. Each one, I know, he thought was the last. He truly delighted in happening upon each of the greetings. All in all, there were about twenty-five of them. When he thought he had them all, he gathered them together and laid them all out on our bathroom counter. Then, it was I who had the surprise of seeing the colorful array in the form of a collage. This note game turned out to be a fun part of the day for us both.

⟫◦⟨

In addition, those entering a room or a house have the obligation to speak first, whether they are your own children or your children's friends or your friends or even you entering a room. A "hello" says, "I'm home."

When children or teenagers leave their friends' homes, it is also their responsibility to say good-bye not only to their friends but to the parents as well. People come and go into the homes of others to visit one person and say neither hello nor good-bye to the other family members. A long conversation with all members is unnecessary, but a short "hello, how are you?" or "Good-bye" is merely the decent thing to do.

Simple household greetings make living so much more pleasant.

The golden years are years, if not decades, away for many of us. Still, if we think about them just a little now, our thoughts and efforts could brighten times for others. Along the way, we will hopefully gain some satisfaction for ourselves.

Many senior citizens have full and healthy lives and enjoy keeping busy with travel, sports and good relationships with friends and family. But many don't.

Keep in mind, that older people need to be kept in touch with by us. They look forward to meaningful contacts from their loved ones and can be disappointed when they are not remembered.

They welcome visits; but if these are not possible because of distance, then calls, letters, floral arrangements on holidays and birthdays, greeting cards or even occasional postcards at any time all help to make a difference in their lives...small touches to let them know you care.

Include them whenever you can in party or holiday celebrations. Plan special events for them, even if it's only a luncheon, tea or get-together for a few friends.

Devoting yourself as such will make life so much more pleasant for them; but you, too, will gain their love, experience and perhaps your own life's perspective in knowing a little more about their past. There are many stories just waiting to be told.

Some older people also need aid with physical or financial concerns. If you are not able to assist them yourself, perhaps locating appropriate assistance for them would be helpful and most appreciated.

If you bake, take a plate of cookies or some cake to them. If you're preparing a casserole for your own dinner, make some extra and present a dish for dinner. If you have leftovers but don't want them yourself, take that over instead. This might be too little for you, but perfect enough a meal for one or two others. I did this often with a neighbor and her husband. Living on a fixed income, she always appreciated and managed to stretch what I gave her to more than one meal. When her husband died, she was even more grateful for these little meals I'd send over. It meant she didn't have to go through the effort of preparing a meal for just one.

As you grow older, reach out to the younger generation. They can help to sustain you in your elder years. There is an old saying that if one does not nurture young friendships now, one might have no friends later.

Visit the sick. A couple of years ago, I had a misfortune transform itself into a good fortune. Suddenly I found myself incapacitated; flat...and I do mean flat...on my back. Not sick, but not able to do, to go, to drive. Not able to sit or walk for more than five minute periods. Not able to move around instinctively as I usually do. Every movement was a conscious decision.

My family, Italian as they are, gather together and actually form a vigil around the sick. They are there whether you want them or not, to give comfort, love and support. They are there to cook meals, clean house and do laundry. They are there to make the sick feel better and to get better soon.

Despite the fact that my grandmother was in a nursing home, her daughters and even her daughter-in-law took turns being with her for seven days a week. I am convinced that this constant vigil and exquisite care is what kept her alive during her last seven years when she died at age 103.

My family was not able to be with me to form this vigil during my incapacitation. Instead, a new family emerged. Busy, turbulent lives aside, my friends took time out to visit me.

Even though most of us are aware and grateful for our good health, often it goes unnoticed and is taken for granted. It is not until we are unable to move around as usual that the true realization of blessed health is appreciated.

Sickness can bring friends together in a form of support which in turn helps in the recovery. If there are no visitors, the sickness can be accompanied by depression and a sense of loneliness. It can also give one a greater appreciation and awareness for the handicapped and the terminally ill.

I became much more aware of the significance and sense of uplifting spirit of a friend stopping by or a simple phone call saying, "How are you?" or a short note or a rainbow of flowers. Because people acted, my life had truly been enriched. Because of these things, my recovery had definitely been sped along. Special people visited me, sent cards, delivered floral arrangements and handheld bouquets, brought lunches we ate together in my bedroom, care baskets of movies, popcorn, magazines, herbal teas, wine, pop and candy and many phone calls checking on me. I knew I had their care, support, concern, love and many offers to help and to do. Yes, they were special people, indeed.

Vital points to keep in mind when visiting the sick:
- Are they up to company?
- Let them regain strength after surgery.
- Check with family, if in doubt.
- Patients do not need to hear about those who've just died or any other negative news.
- Only visit during visiting hours.
- Visitor stays should be brief.

A gracious lady. The most gracious people try to give their undivided attention despite their busy schedules. One such lady is a number one pro at it. Former director of a private elementary and middle school, Jane's hours every day were filled to capacity. Yet, when someone needed her, she was *totally* there for them. She did not get harried, nor did she hurry. She welcomed one and all into her office and she listened. Her quiet calm and easy going, gracious manner would have led one to believe she had nothing else to do. I always marveled at her calm in the face of the zillion things on her schedule.

The art of letter-writing. Another fancy letter arrived for me today. The handwriting was so perfect that at first glance, it appeared to be one of those pre-written, copied advertisements. Upon closer scrutiny, though, it became evident that this was indeed an original, fancy-scrolled, handwritten letter. A letter written with a fountain pen, no less. Imagine. A fountain pen, in this day of felt-tipped markers and ball point pens.

A letter written with a good fountain pen is a delight to behold. Liquid ink, that from a fountain pen, tends to flow more evenly and smoothly, and with less pressure over a page than ballpoint ink. You say, dip into an old fashioned inkwell? Not necessarily. Ink filled cartridges are available.

Not long ago, I had the sheer luxury of reading several letters written in the early 1940s by a young woman, my late mother-in-law, Grace Fitzgerald, to her younger brother, Joe, then in the service during World War II. They were sincere, old-fashioned letters which brought home to Joe in a faraway land. I could hardly know what it was like to have a loved one so far away, but in reading those letters some forty years later, I truly felt the love pouring out and the sense of family she wanted him to remember. Oh, and how very much she missed him.

The letters were peppered with the activities of those at home, news of daily happenings and even some humor. She listened to the war news every day and related whatever she'd heard. This young girl knew how to write a letter and I know Joe must have devoured and savored every one of them.

A letter, you know, is really talk on paper. If you can carry a conversation on the telephone, you can write a letter. Yes, you can. Don't think about what you're going to write. Just write. You say you don't have anything to say? Not to worry. The words will flow as though they are actually coming from the pen instead of from your mind. Don't strain; let them flow naturally, informally, as you would talk them. By the way, no one will ever know how long you searched for just the right word.

Sometimes a telephone call can be an imposition. A personal letter is the next best thing to a visit, and the really neat thing is that you can re-live that visit by re-reading the letter. Once, twice or even more.

Make someone happy. Write a letter and let them know you are thinking of them. After not having done so in several months, I picked up pen and paper and jotted a note to dear eighty-five year old Peggy in another state. The following week I received an answer from her. This is how her letter opened: "Dear Carol,

54

You have no idea how happy you made me today when I received your letter. I think of you real often..." Her opening statement, in turn, gave me a glow to think that a small gesture of the note on my part made her feel so good. If you haven't made contact with a friend lately, write a letter.

Get back in the habit of letter writing. Or if you've never been in the habit, develop it. Writing a letter isn't so hard. And besides, a letter can be read whenever the recipient has time and can be saved and savored.

As with thank you notes, half the battle is having the proper tools and a place to write. If you have a writing desk, keep paper, pens, stamps and addresses in a basket or caddy on the desk. Then all you have to do is sit and start. Even if you don't have a desk, keep all of the writing paraphernalia in a basket or decorative box. Retrieve it whenever you're ready and find a comfortable spot whether it is at your kitchen or dining room table or curled up on the sofa or in bed with a lap desk.

———◆———

At least once a day I hear, "Was there any mail for me?" Mail is also one of the highlights of my day. As I retrieve it from the mailbox, I always scan through the junk and the bills, looking for something just for me, happy when I find it. After I've pitched the junk and tucked the bills, I then find a proper place for myself, settle in and happily read these notes addressed only to me. Sometimes the words are sad and I cry as I did when Charmaine told me how her mother, a special caretaker of my babies, had suffered in the end and how she, Charmaine, had not even one day with her husband alone as her mother had always lived with them and how now, Charmaine's husband was very ill, suffering much and dying. My heart went out to Charmaine and I grieved for her and her mother. I read that letter over and over again. Yes, sometimes the letters are sad but above all, they are special and they carry with them love and friendship. They carry with them caring and sharing of ourselves. These are special lasting gifts that we can enjoy time and time again.

If you are still in doubt as to what to write, read an excerpt of what Lord Chesterfield said two centuries ago as his letter began:

Dear Boy,
"When you write to me, suppose yourself conversing freely with me by the fireside. In that case, you would naturally mention the incidents of the day: as where you had been, whom you had seen, what you thought of them, and so forth. Do this in your letters! Acquaint me sometimes with your diversions; tell me of any new persons or characters that you meet in company; and add your own observations upon them. In short, let me see more of you in your letters."

Now that we know what to write, how many of us actually have the time for lengthy letters, let alone fancy handwriting and fountain pens? While some experts

56

will tell you it is only socially correct to pen a letter, I've always maintained that a nicely typed letter is quicker and still very much welcomed over a hurriedly scribbled letter that others might have to strain to decipher. Having to manage through it once, one might not even consider giving it a second reading. Not to mention how much longer it takes to write than to type. So, if handwriting is holding you back, go ahead and type a letter. Then sign your name.

If you're interested in developing a pen pal, write to the International Pen Friends, P.O. Box 2900 65, Brooklyn, New York 11229-0001. Send a self-addressed stamped envelope and you will receive a list of 14 names of people who are in your age group and share your interests. There are 300,000 International Pen Friend Members in 156 countries.

Here's another one: Golden Pen-Pal Association of North America. Send a self-addressed stamped envelope to golden Pen-Pal Association of North America,1304 Hedgelawn Way, Raleigh, North Carolina 27615.

So as you think of giving, give an expression of yourself by sending a personal letter, whether written or typed, whether to a friend or to a stranger. In these days of the hurry-up syndrome when many have lost sight of this old-fashioned form of communication, making a special point to send a letter is something that will surely be appreciated. A great way to keep in touch.

Writing letters does a few things:

• It keeps you in constant contact with good friends and loved ones no matter what your geographical distance is.

• As mentioned earlier, unlike phone calls, the letters can be read and re-read and savored each time, and can also be saved as keepsakes.

• You can be kept up-to-date on the happenings and goings-on in the lives of those you care about.

• It gives the recuperating, the retiring and the lonely something to look forward to knowing someone cares.

• It lets you know you are being thought about; conversely, you are letting others know you are thinking of them...Keeps you close in mind and heart.

> **Sir Philip Sidney said it this way:**
> *"Fool"* **said my muse to me,**
> *"Look in thy heart and write."*

> Charles Dickens once wrote,
> "She'll wish there was more, and
> that's the great art o'letter-writin'."

And after reading all of the foregoing and you are still turned off to letter writing, then send an audio or video cassette. But, on a regular basis, do keep in touch with those you love.

Speaking of videos, I know someone who had her special gathering of 25 videotaped with each one offering their say about what the holiday meant to them. It was set to music and the end was edited in a unique way that singled out each person. She had copies made and sent them to her family as gifts. They were warmly touched to watch this precious remembrance and keepsake of a special time.

Part Two

Preserve Your Sanity So You Don't Lose Your Mind!

This segment of the book makes recommendations and suggestions for how to stay sane. How to maintain good feelings and how to reduce stress. In it you will find:

Ways to make yourself feel good
Ways to make yourself feel important
Inspiration for "keeping on" when times are tough

Ways to create order and organization
How to be grateful
The importance of making lists
How to set appointments so the anxiety is reduced

Reducing anxiety in general
How to get your point across without arguing

Many ways on how to keep and be more organized

Many ponderable moments on preserving your sense of balance

Don't quit when the odds are against you. Put one foot in front of the other and keep moving. As the line in the movie, "Steel Magnolias" says, *If it doesn't kill you, it'll make you stronger.*

Weigh in everyday even though there is much information contrary to this idea. I have a better grip on my weight when I know exactly where I am in relation to the scales. If you find that you are two or three pounds up, cut back for a few days, rather than waiting until it has gotten out of hand and overwhelming.

Eat at least three meals a day or more if they're small. For years, I skipped two in an effort to maintain my weight. As I grew older, I found that I needed more. Not only did I *need* more, but I also *wanted* more. Bread that is thirty-five to forty calories per slice will enable you to have two slices of French toast in the morning and a whole sandwich for lunch. Bread was practically non-existent in my diet. Sandwiches and potatoes too. A baked potato for dinner and low calorie bread are now in my diet daily and my weight is still manageable. Besides, the Food Pyramid put out by the FDA now suggests six to eleven servings of grains per day. If you read labels and buy low-fat or non-fat most of the time, then when you do get the urge to splurge, you can do so from time to time and it won't devastate you. A good combination of calorie watching and low fat foods is a must. One exclusive of the other is not enough. Keep in mind, that our bodies do need a certain amount of fat intake so everything works together properly.

If you are in a rut, climb out of it. If life is boring to you, find different ways of doing things so it doesn't become so routine. There is no reason to live dull, unexciting, mundane, ordinary lives. Refuse to be bored. Do something! Call a friend. Go out to lunch. Create a poem. Yes. Even if you've never done so before. Feed your mind: Read. Try a new recipe. Invite someone for dinner.  Go to a movie. No one to go with? Go alone. Draw. Paint. Go back to school. Learn about yourself: Take a personality test. Do a family tree. Go window shopping. Browse through a book store. Go to a spa. Change your hairstyle. Wear a new color. Wear a hat. Go to a concert in the park. Volunteer at the hospital. Join a choir. Go apple picking. When you get home,  bake an apple pie. Yum! Build a snowman. Walk in the rain. Fly a kite - it's one of my childhood memories. Write a long letter to each of your children, young or adult, recalling special events or times in their lives and letting them know how precious they are. Choose one of the above or find your own. Just do it!

⟫◦⟪

Or how about this? Leave a legacy for your children or grandchildren. Leave them some wonderful memories by writing your life story, your memoirs. Everyone has a story to tell. No matter how ordinary, we're all unique. We've all accumulated a vast store of experiences: paths we've followed, people who have enriched our lives, happy times, sad times, accomplishments, humorous incidents, poignant happenings and many other memories just waiting to be tapped. Once we're gone, so are our memories...unless we decide to leave them.

Just like love, the richness of our family stories become richer everytime we share them. This past holiday, I heard some wonderful stories, for the very first time, from my father who is 87 years old. I was touched by hearing them and a little surprised that after all these years, I was learning some things I'd never heard before. Our memories are more wonderful than anyone can imagine. And we all have the potential to remember our past. Sometimes we can conjure up our own memories of things we've done, places we've been and people in our lives. Sometimes these memories encroach unbidden at the sound of a song or a familiar smell.

There are books on this subject. Go to your library and find them. Here is one for a start, *How to Write Your Life Story* by Frank Thomas. You won't be wondering how or what once you've read this book. He gives many examples and idea starters. What better gift? For others or yourself. But before you get to the library, here are thirteen brain-joggers to start you:

- Little stories. Think back about various incidents that have happened in your life. Write them down.
- Humor. Find something funny that either

affects you or someone else. Or amusing things your children did or said.

• Baby Books. If you recorded in these books, go back and look at what you wrote. You'll recall the events as they happened. Then you can enlarge upon them.

• In your opinion, what makes someone a winner? What makes you or your family winners?

• How good are your coping skills?

• Did you have a nickname while growing up. How did you come by it? How did it affect you in areas of your life?

• What is the one thing that remains a mystery to you?

• Write about why you are proud of your children. What good qualities do your children have?

• Think back to when you first started dating? What are your all-time favorite memories?

• At what age did you get your first car? How much did it cost? What kind was it? How did you learn to drive?

• What about your first job? What was it? How much pay did you receive?

• Describe a time in your life that you consider was your absolute finest?

• Interview your mother and father, your grandparents, aunts and uncles and get these stories recorded before it's too late.

By now you're probably thinking, *that's a huge project. I don't have time for anything like that!* Think again. Take fifteen minutes a day, yes just fifteen, and write a paragraph (or talk into a tape recorder) about some facet of your life. Don't go on and on. Just a paragraph. These fifteen minute paragraphs at the end of a larger block of time will be the basis for your story.

Remember bits of time add up to chunks. If you're waiting for huge chunks of uninterrupted time for this project or any other you've been wanting to start, they may never come, and consequently your project may never get started, let alone completed. Wait no more! Grab whatever free minutes are available and begin. Once you've started, the next attempt at it will be easier. On long car trips or those chauffeuring waiting times, or while you're watching water boil, at long red lights, or even standing in line at the grocery store. A few minutes here, a few minutes there and before you know it, you're through or at least well on your way to a finished project. I couldn't have accomplished writing this book without doing a little at a time.

One by one. When you're feeling overwhelmed with a zillion things to do, think about Mother Teresa when asked how she does it all. "One by one" was her answer.

Treat yourself with Kid gloves. I know women and mothers who accept verbal and mental abuse from their husbands and their children. Don't even *think* about tolerating it. It is totally unacceptable.

Feeling good. I *feel* good when my surroundings are attractive and pleasing to my eye. I *feel* good when things are orderly. Conversely, I feel disjointed and not right with the world when things are strewn about helter skelter. If you are feeling out of sorts, perhaps your surroundings are making you frustrated and irritable.

What makes you feel good? Find whatever it is. Something as small as a mailbox perked up my days. Every time I backed out of my new driveway, I saw an ugly, metal, rusty mailbox. Every time I drove into my driveway, I saw the same ugly, metal, rusty mailbox. Each time I eyed that unpleasant sight, I did not feel good. Too many times. Until finally, one day, I decided to change it. Later, I saw a tee-shirt that read, "Life is how you change it." Anyway, I went to the hardware store and bought a white wooden post, a white mail box and a decorative finial for the top of the post. A very simple change. But now, whenever I back out of my driveway and into it again I see something that makes me feel good. The entire purchase probably cost under twelve dollars. Well worth it for a much improved mental outlook.

Similarly, after we moved into our house, I lived with drapes that, to me, were "ugly". They were not me, nor were they my style. They gave me no pleasure; rather they sapped my energy and made me feel uncomfortable each time I looked at them. When I could stand them no longer, down they came in one fell swoop. The window was bare, but *nothing* was suddenly better than the *wrong* thing. Ask yourself if you settle for the wrong thing.

Mornings. I love to *be* up early in the morning. Notice I did not say *get* up. *Getting* up early is a real chore. I've often thought, 'if there was only some other way to start the day, than getting up...' So. my clock is set thirty minutes ahead. When my mental alarm (that's what time I tell myself I need to awaken) wakes me, I really have another thirty minutes to gradually climb out of my slumber before I actually need to set a foot on the floor. It takes that long just to open my eyes. And I'd rather open them *before* I start navigating rather than *while* I navigate. So those few extra minutes work for me. Once I'm up, my energy is untold and I tackle a multitude of things in a day. I've spoken to several retirees who say one of the biggest enjoyments they have is waking up naturally rather than bolting out of bed in half a stupor. There are people who need a siren to wake them. There are those who merely need an alarm clock or radio. And yet, there is the other faction that rely on their biological clocks. What kind of riser are you? Can you make it any easier on yourself?

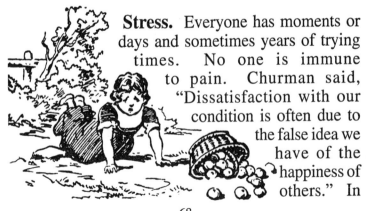

Stress. Everyone has moments or days and sometimes years of trying times. No one is immune to pain. Churman said, "Dissatisfaction with our condition is often due to the false idea we have of the happiness of others." In other words, too often people compare their insides with others' outsides. It's safer not to compare.

During some of my difficult times, people have asked me how I was able to get through it. My answer was, "I walked, I shopped, I talked, I wrote, I read and I baked. My cookie jar was never empty. Mostly I tend to bake when things bother me and even when they don't, but I, for one, need to keep busy. That doesn't mean ignoring a situation or brushing it under the rug. But if it is something that cannot be changed, you need to find an outlet for how you feel about it.

> *God, grant me the serenity to*
> *Accept the things I cannot change*
> *The courage to change the things I can*
> *And the wisdom to know the difference*

How do you handle yourself during times of stress? For starters, you could practice the above prayer. If you choose to 'talk', do you know your listener? Information could boomerang if told to the wrong person. But sometimes hearing yourself verbalize suddenly opens up answers you hadn't thought about before. The mere act of writing is therapy in itself. If you are angry with someone, write to them. Usually the anger seems to dissipate and mailing the letter is no longer even necessary. Write down your feelings. Write about your problems. It's amazing that answers seem to arise just by putting pen to paper or by verbalizing your concerns. Or try taping a message into a recorder, then play it back and see how you feel. When you are upset or angry, a long, brisk walk helps too. You'd be surprised how much calmer you are when you return. And whether you know it or not, you will have made a step in reducing your stress.

Keep in mind that stress is not only negative things around you. Even good things such as moving, having a baby, starting a new job, planning a wedding or entertaining can also be stressful.

When our daughter Keri, now 24, was given a pre-kindergarten test, we were told that she *monitored her own behavior.* She didn't frustrate herself by pushing to do something she knew she couldn't do. Over the years, we witnessed this concept many times. Some people try and keep trying and never know when something is too difficult or too much for them. Consequently, frustration sets in. Do you monitor your behavior? Or do you wear yourself to a frazzle going to and fro, trying to please everyone? This is not to be confused with quitting, rather knowing when to say no and when to say yes; when to go forward and when to pull back; when to say, *I can do more* and when to say, *I've had enough.*

—————

Now try this exercise: Make a list of the things that are invading your serenity. Is it your job? Your spouse? Your financial situation? Is it your children? List them all. Now, put a star by everything you can't possibly do anything about and pray to accept those things. Next, number all the items that you feel are changeable. Number them in order of priority. Now, start to work on changing them. Not all at once. Just one at a time. Put at the top of the list to get your proper rest so you can feel good. Then start tackling the remainder on your list and begin a change.

> *If you worry, why pray?*
> *If you pray, why worry?*

Learn to say no. Give no excuses. Just nicely decline. And let go of the guilt. This, too, is imperative for your peace of mind if you are always saying yes and running in ten different directions all at the same time. Sometimes we *must* say yes for the good of all, when we would rather say no, but generally many people say yes to the detriment of their own mental and physical well-being, and then complain about it to boot. If you choose to say yes when you'd rather say no, then for pete's sake, don't utter one negative word about it!

Balancing time. Enjoy your friends and your family but guard your space...and your privacy. Your mental health relies on it. Enjoy delicious moments alone whenever you can. If that's impossible in your house, go for a walk. Choose the prettiest part of town. If you're near a beach or a lake path, enjoy the nature. Hear the quiet. Do it!

Or here's another thought: Rather than have a babysitter come in so you can go out, have a babysitter or your spouse take the children out so you can stay in. It is seldom that mothers have the opportunity to be in their own home...alone.

If you spend too much time alone, and you need company, then seek that out as well. Begin to invite people in on a regular basis. If a dinner is more than you'd care to do, try a brunch or lunch. Or invite friends for cards or scrabble, then dessert and coffee. Don't dwell on your aloneness. Get out of the house if you have to push yourself out. One woman I know said her family nudged her out. She was spending too much time alone and feeling depressed much of that time. Now, she is enjoying classes, volunteering and a myriad of activities. You're only alone if you want to be.

Being alone allows one time to pause, to reflect, ponder, meditate and let the quiet speak to you. But as much as I enjoy my quiet times, my soul and very being craves my friends and family as well. Too much of one or the other, though, creates tension within me. I need a balance of the two.

Lists. I've always been teased for my list making. But it's the only way I can feel organized and actually remember all that I want or need to do. One feature of making lists for me is the feeling of exhilaration that comes when I cross off things as they are finished. If you need to sense accomplishment, this small act may be worth it. If you have several errands to make around town, perhaps you could do the one farthest from your home first, and work your way to the stops near your home at the end of your journey. Makes more sense than to back track or to move in circles. Making lists is a major time-saver and a valuable organizational tool. Making lists is automatic for me. But I realize that it doesn't come so naturally to some, my Bill for one. He has a dickens of a time making a list and sticking to it. If you fall into that category, try just putting three items a day on your list. No more. I repeat, no more. Just three. Try following that pattern for awhile. If your tendency is to list more, you may just get frustrated and quit before your deeds get accomplished.

Telephones. Early in our marriage, we were visiting an older couple in another city. The phone rang while we were there. Dick and Bill and I were sitting at the dining room table while Lorraine was on her way to the other end of the house. The phone rang. Lorraine continued the direction she was going. Dick made no move to grab the phone and there was no one else in the house. I sat there astounded as the phone continued to ring. Finally, I said, "Isn't anyone going to answer the phone?" Dick nonchalantly said, "Lorraine will if it's still ringing when she comes back this direction." I found this attitude totally shocking and foreign, for up until that time and as a teenager, we had literally pounced on a ringing telephone, sometimes two or three of us at once.

On the other hand, I also found this way of thinking very refreshing. From that day on, I never broke my neck to get to the phone, nor do I let it interfere with my peace of mind or frustrate me. As necessary a wonderful invention it is, sometimes it can drive a body crazy. Though answering machines today have pretty much given us the space we need. If you don't have a recorder, use the phone when necessary, but don't let it dominate your life. It can waste your time and keep you from doing what's on your daily list.

Take a break. If you've been working for a long

stretch, offer yourself a break. Then take it.

Refuse to be a part of negative attitudes. Surround yourself with talented, intelligent people. Avoid the complainers and the whiners. Spend time with people who like to laugh.

Lighten up. "The art of being wise is the art of knowing what to overlook," says William James. Keep your own frustration at a low level by knowing what to overlook, and asking yourself, *how important is it?*

Utilize your waiting time. Carry notepaper and stamps with you. Catch up on some correspondence while you wait for appointments or for children in carpools. Keep some reading material in the car. Put 3 x 5 index cards in your purse or post-it notes on the seat next to you in the car. Use these to jot quick notes or reminders to yourself. Your waiting time won't seem so formidable and you'll actually be putting time to good use instead of gritting your teeth or biting your fingernails.

Be prepared. Also good to keep in the car is a box of tissue. In the glove compartment, have a ready supply of pens, napkins, and scotch tape. Scotch tape in the glove compartment you ask? Have you ever had to rush out at the last minute to buy a child's birthday gift? Now, instead of running home to wrap it, save a trip. Wrap it in the car after your purchase and drop off with your child to the birthday house. Also convenient in the glove compartment are cotton-tips and individually wrapped wetwipes. These come in handy on the way to school in the morning and when stopping for fast food at the drive-through.

Brighten up your workspace. You know how the children use book covers to protect their school books? Well, you could do the same with your dictionary and other reference books. Instead, use a floral paper or a pattern to suit your tastes. Imported papers are another thought. Or how about leftover wallpaper.

Let go. When you or someone you know is striving to know the outcome to a situation or an answer to a problem that isn't fast in coming, adopt the attitude of our friend, Charlie. When he is approached with questions from others regarding unknown answers, his apt response is, "Well, one thing is sure. We'll know more later!" In other words, don't beat your head against a brick wall trying to force an answer or a solution. Let go of it for awhile. The answer will be there eventually and sometimes when you least expect it.

Rid all the *shoulds* and *have tos* from your vocabulary. They only heap unnecessary guilt on you. Not good for your mental health.

Slow down. I mean *really* slow down.

> Will Durant says: "No man who is in a hurry is quite civilized."

Naturally, sometimes we all hurry. But think about it

and do whatever you can to keep yourself from constantly being in a rush. Certainly does not add to a good mental frame of mind. In fact, it usually does just the opposite by creating lots of stress and anxiety.

Need and want. My good friend, Anne, says, "Sometimes you need the things you want more than the things you need." Think about it.

Don't complain. I mean on a regular basis. You can't help complaining about some of things some of the time. It's the continual complaining to which I refer. If you can just try to be aware and when you get the urge, replace the thought with a note of thanks, instead. It's amazing what this will do for your spirit.

Noise. In busy households with many people coming and going, the television plays an ever present role. So does music from the children's room so that sometimes everyone else's noise is all you hear. When you have the house to yourself, savor the quiet. Or better yet, seize the opportunity to play *your* music.

Relieve your pressure. During a three year period, pressure had built within me twice. Both times it finagled its way into my back. The first time, I was only incapacitated for a week. The second time, I was totally out of commission for three full weeks and eventually had to have surgery. I know, beyond the shadow of a doubt, that stress did me in. Phil Barnhart said it succinctly in one of his newsletters. He recalled a line from the movie, "Godfather III" where one of the characters said, *The mind suffers and the body cries out.*

Wow! How true! Phil likened that quote to the definition of psychosomatic illness. He went on to say, "The body knows what the mind tells it. When the body hears the negative and the detrimental, it becomes offended, gets nervous, and then sick. Sometimes it dies from an overdose of bad news. But the converse of that is also true. If there is psychosomatic illness, there is psychosomatic health. If we can talk ourselves into illness, we can talk ourselves into wellness."

We cannot be effective or productive if we are constantly under pressure. A thumb or finger that's been slammed in a door sometimes needs to be drilled so the blood doesn't build up. A tire with too much air will eventually pop. A body with too much stress will become physically ill or mentally overwrought. Relieve your pressure before you burst! (Refer to the serenity exercise on p. 69) Or just have a good cry.

Albert Smith said,
*"Tears are the safety valve
of the heart
when too much pressure
is laid on it."*

Then again, you could kick stress by the very idea of forgetting. Reflect on this:

Forget the slander you have heard,
Forget the hasty, unkind word;
Forget the quarrel and the cause,
Forget the whole affair, because
Forgetting is the only way.
Forget the storm of yesterday,
Forget the chap whose sour face
Forgets to smile in any place.
Forget you're not a millionaire
Forget the gray streaks in your hair.
Forget the coffee when it's cold
Forget to kick, forget to scold,
Forget the plumber's awful charge,
Forget the iceman's bill is large;
Forget the coalman and his ways,
Forget the winter's blustery days.

Anonymous

Pray for your spouse. Pray for your marriage. Pray for your relationship with each other.

Be grateful. I mean really grateful. Make a list of these things in your life. Keep the list going. Start with: You have a roof over your head. It doesn't leak. You are happily married. You are happily divorced. You have your health. If you've been ill, practice psychosomatic wellness. You have a bed to climb into at night. You know, things like that. Write them all down.

A quiet argument. If you must indulge in arguing, at least do so with a quiet voice. You can probably get your point across better if you don't yell.

> Remember:
> *A soft answer
> turneth away wrath.*

Appointments. I usually opt for appointments later in the day. I also usually find myself waiting. A friend told me she likes to take the first appointment in the morning to avoid these very waits. A new thought! I tried it. My most recent appointment was at 7:00 a.m. I was called in to the office by 7:10 a.m. and home to start my day before eight. I had been to the doctor and home again and the day was still fresh. If you do find yourself waiting, have needlework, a letter or some reading material with you. You won't feel as though your waiting time was wasted time.

Save mental anxiety. Do you get crabby when you reach for a kitchen or toiletry item and then find you have run out? Keep a shopping list handy and jot these items down as you see they are running low... *before* you run out. Train others in your household to do the same.

For quick household jobs or changing the location of a picture, keep a hammer, picture hooks, a few nails, a screw driver and a pliers handy in one of your kitchen drawers. This is only for your use. The main tools will be in the garage or the basement. Saves you steps and will probably always be there when you need it if you are the only one to use it.

Have another nearby spot for scotch tape, ruler, scissor, pens, pencils and message paper. Train all those who use them to replace when finished, so they are there for the next user.

Lather your tired feet. Do your feet burn and ache after being on them for hours? Before you climb into bed, massage them with lotion, any kind. They'll feel good as new in the morning.

Bring to mind your own good qualities. Sometimes our brain likes to tell us of our negatives, but by focusing, you'd be surprised how many positives you also have. Here is an exercise, good for self-awareness: Get a sheet of paper, draw a line down the center. Head one side, *Things I like about myself* and the other side, *Things I don't like about myself.* In the appropriate column, start listing such things as I'm punctual, caring, sensitive, responsible, helpful, tardy, angry, lazy, hardworking, patient, impatient, funny. Think of others and keep listing. What you have listed, will tell you what areas you may want to improve or it may tell you things you hadn't consciously thought about yourself.

⟫•◦•⟪

Part Three

*Move Forward
So You Don't
Fall Backward*

⟫•◦•⟪

There is no such thing as standing still. We either move ahead or lag behind. So if you don't work to improve yourself, you will decline.

Many ideas in this section aim toward being a better person and include the following concepts:

Change your attitude
Be a good friend
Exercise
Listen to yourself
Listen to others
Don't expect perfection
Communicate
Read
Inner and outer rejuvenation
Learn - educate yourself
Be aware
Make-up
Invitations
Enlist help
Improve your memory

⟫•◦•⟪

Try this. Say "Sure" without hesitating or grumbling when asked by your spouse or your children to do something for them, such as, "Will you get me a glass of water?" or "Can you help me with this project?" or "Will you give me a ride to school?" In an effort to be gentle, cheerful and helpful, I said this many times with our fifth and youngest child, Mary Carol. Over the years, it became a built-in response with her when others ask her for a favor. So much the nicer, than the attitude of "do it" or "get it yourself".

"A laugh is worth a hundred groans in any market," says Charles Lamb.

Don't spill confidential information. Not even a little bit.

Exercise. If this is not your very favorite thing to do as in my case, at least try a twenty minute walk three or four times a week. It's better than nothing.

Surround yourself with people from whom you can learn. We all know people who energize us. Then, there are those who can just as easily sap our energy. Do you also find there are people who bring out the worst in you? What about yourself? Are you the type who brings out the best or the worst in others?

"I love you, not only for what you are, but for what I am when I am with you."

Do the best that you can in any endeavor you undertake, but don't chastise yourself if you haven't done it perfectly. Don't even begin to strive for perfection. You only set yourself up for disappointment when you do.

Lose yourself in a good book. If you don't have time to wade through a book only to find out it is not your taste, ask others you respect to recommend a good read.

Don't expect anyone, especially your spouse or your children, to know what you are thinking. Communicate it in words...or pictures or notes or letters or something else creatively done.

Attend your reunions. I went to my first five-year class reunion and then did not go back until my thirtieth. I thoroughly enjoyed it and you too may find them to be wonderfully refreshing as you meet friends from long ago. Studies have shown that those who've made the decision to go are glad they did. Whether it's a family, school or military reunion there's planning help available. For a free guide, call 1-800-447-7300. It's filled with all the details you'll need to get your group together.

Refurbish your shoes. Tacky is: wearing scuffed shoes with worn down heels. We have friends who remove their shoes each time they come in from an outing. Then, they put them directly across the hall from the garage entrance in the laundry room. Those shoes are wiped and polished before they are worn again. Shoes always look great and it certainly saves on their floors and carpeting. Be aware of how your foot rests on the accelerator when you drive. As your heel touches the floor, it also collects a big black smudge.

Put a lilt in your voice the next time you answer your telephone.

Tidy your house not only when guests come, but also for yourself.

Smile. "A man without a smiling face must not open up shop," says an ancient Chinese proverb. Even by today's standards, a smile can do wondrous things: It can endear the most disagreeable looking people, it has been known to vanquish many a quarrel, sometimes better than words, it can make a connection and send a message. A smile communicates vital information: It can win over the most cantankerous person. It can welcome people, make them feel good and can even lend some comfort.

Scientific studies have shown that as people watched faces expressing pain they, too, felt distress. Wouldn't this hold true if people saw more smiles? Would they have more good feelings as well? So, lighten up and Smile!

Watch your posture. Stand up straight. Feet together. Notice how many women stand with feet apart. Not attractive.

Check yourself in a full length mirror before leaving the house.

Eating a snack. Just an idea, but instead of standing in the kitchen eating a half-peeled banana, slice it onto a plate, sprinkle with cinnamon, sit at the table and eat with a fork.

Clean your purse regularly, as in every few days! Pitch the garbage, gather the change from the bottom and file your tax receipts. If you can find a purse with compartments or a separate purse organizer with sections, keeping a neat purse will be much easier.

Find a comfortable spot: the beach, your bedroom, a cozy chair in your living room, the park or the library. Then read. And read and read. Not long ago, I had a deadline for some reading I needed to finish. I was having difficulty accomplishing it at home. Too many other things invading my time. Determined to complete it, I hopped in the car, drove to the library, went to the farthest corner with my back to any activity and there in two hours I finished.

Is your marriage good, but you would like to make it better? Go to a Worldwide Marriage Encounter.

Remember this: "...academic achievement is the one accomplishment that no one can ever destroy and that nothing can ever erode." Some people will tell you that it's not that important. I went back to college to finish my degree when I was 42. With five children still at home. Yes it was hard. And there were times I never thought I'd get it all done. But if I had it to do over, I definitely would! So! If you want to go back to school for the mere sake of sensing an accomplishment and boosting your self-esteem, do it. If you want to go back because you want or need a career, you're never too old. I did it the traditional way because I was only twenty minutes from a college campus. But if you can't afford the time away from home to sit in a classroom, there are non-traditional Bachelor, Masters and Doctorate degrees available through correspondence courses. One such place is Columbia Pacific University, 1415 Third Street, San Rafael, California 94901. Write to them if you're interested. Other sources: *How to Get the Degree You Want (formerly Bear's Guide to Non- Traditional College Degrees)* by John B. Bear, *Worldwide Educational Directory* by Mohammad S. Mirza, *Innovative Graduate Programs Directory*-Empire State College, and *The Correspondence Educational Directory* by John Harding Jones.

The English have a word for it: Ramble. Set out on foot to discover some gems, hidden when you're in a car. The English consider walking an art form. Why, they even have books on the subject. Whether you opt for a stroll in solitude or plan one with a friend you might try reading *Literary Walks of Britain or Shank's Mare*. Then, leave your keys at home for a change, and do what the English do. Ramble. You might discover some charming treasures.

Check it. If you are a poor speller, use a dictionary. Or best to have another pair of eyes proof-read your work. It's easy to skim right over our own errors because we read what's meant to be there instead of what's there, missing the actual errors. The height of unprofessionalism is to send out correspondence with misspelled words and grammatical errors. Occasionally, typographical errors do sneak through but I once received an advertisement for a new business in town and in five small paragraphs, there were eleven misspelled words. I, and many others like me, don't look for these errors, they actually leap off the page and dance before our very eyes.

Starting the day. Living in a two story house for many years, I found early in my marriage that if I went downstairs *before* getting dressed, I would get very involved in doing a thousand things before I ever made my way back upstairs to dress for the day.

Thus, I always made it a point to make my bed as I climbed out of it and to dress completely (make-up, hair combed and all) before I set about my day. I was ready to dash out if I needed to or ready to welcome drop-in company if the doorbell rang. With children? Yes, especially with children. Babies and small children can demand all day. Take your time in the morning (even if it means getting up earlier) or you may never get it the rest of the day. And not getting those few minutes to tend to ourselves can be one of the quirky things that makes us not feel good, and can set the tone for the rest of the day.

Consider each day a gift and don't put off anything. Do what you've been putting off. Make that intended call. Buy a rose and visit your friend in the hospital. Bill met someone recently who told him that when he had heart surgery, he had not one visitor, not even from his daughter who lived in the same town.

Make-up. Take a good sharp look in the mirror. It has been said that if we *look* good, we also *feel* good. Learn to put on make-up the right way. If you have the inclination, go to a department store cosmetic counter or go to a make-up artist. They have the talent and the training to instruct and apply make-up to the myriad of imperfections we possess. They use tricks and special illusions and they are able to compensate for *and* camouflage the defects while focusing on other more salient features of the face.

"The look and shape of the eyebrows are terribly important," explains Linda Cohoon, founder and owner of Bright Future Make-Up Studio in Chicago, "and women in general do not know what the construction of the brow should be for their shaped face. The right eyebrow arch can enhance or detract from your face," she says.

Also new on the market is permanent make-up. Eyebrows, eyeliner, and even lip color. This would certainly save time and you'd always be ready to go.

But do research this concept before you decide if it's right for you. Permanent means forever.

Good skin care means removing make-up nightly. That is, *every* night. Develop your own ritual, but do develop one.

Being tidy. When things around me are messy, I tend to become confused, not knowing what to do first and sometimes I end up spinning my wheels. If I feel I haven't accomplished much, then I become out of sorts. Try to keep your work area tidy so you can work better. Many times I have seen people pick up one stack of papers, then another and another in an effort to locate something specific. I've done it myself. Sound familiar? It's a real waste of time, not to mention energy to continually handle the same pieces of paper searching for what we need. I can't be productive if I'm not efficient. So I've put myself in the habit of using file folders instead of stacks of papers, even if it's  only for one item. Do you need to have someone help you *get* organized? If so, it might be easier to *stay* organized.

Try not to interrupt. This is something that practically everybody does at one time or another. The point here is to be aware. If you do have this tendency and really must get your point in, when you've finished your thought, at least be kind enough to apologize and remind the person you interrupted to go on with what they were saying.

What kind of a listener are you? Don't usurp a conversation. You'll be interesting, if you are interested. Listen fully when others are speaking. Wait until they are finished before you speak. Your questions may be answered and usually are, before you need to ask them. I have been in groups and classes where people have interrupted to ask questions. If they had been listening intently, they would have known their question had already been answered.

My late father-in-law, Edward Fitzgerald, used to say, "It is far better to remain still and *appear* ignorant, than to open your mouth and remove all doubt." That isn't to be confused with not asking legitimate questions for fear of "looking dumb." For, *the only dumb question is the one that's never asked.* And who knows, others may have the same questions on their minds.

> An American Indian proverb states: "Listen, or thy tongue will keep thee deaf".

Listen to yourself. The more excited I get, the higher the pitch of my voice. As soon as I hear the stridency, I try to take a deep breath and tone down with the next word.

Invitations: They help contribute to our social well-being. We all need a little fun in our lives to balance the sometimes ordinary-ness of the work week. Repondez s'il vous plait, better know as R.S.V.P., French words used all over the world, most often seen in the lower left hand corner of an invitation. In general, this says, please respond to our invitation. R.S.V.P. does not mean a casual reply if you feel like it. It means you are obligated to let your hosts know whether or not you will be able to attend the event to which you have been invited. It is an honor to receive an invitation. It should be honored with a prompt reply which also keeps you in good stead with your hostess. Be sure your children respond to their invitations as well. It's a common courtesy.

A handshake conveys an attitude about you. It can say you are confident or insecure, friendly or blasé. Children seem to enjoy shaking hands and should be taught at an early age the proper way: a good firm grip, not too loose, not tight. As I've told them in my classes: *no wet fishes, no bone crushers.* Clasp the whole hand (not half which sometimes happens), and look the other person in the eye, as you greet them with a warm smile.

Did you know that ages ago, the right hand reached for the sword during warring times. Extending it has always meant friendly greetings during peaceful times.

Count to ten. When you feel like lashing out, cover your mouth. For as Charles Spurgeon says, "Love stands in the presence of a fault with a finger on its lip." Also remember that "Patience is the ability to idle your motor when you feel like stripping your gears." And try this one: "Swallowing angry words is a lot easier than having to eat them."

Ask for help. Do you do everything yourself in your house? Stop! When there are four, five, or six or more people living in a house, the load is too much for one person. Start enlisting the help of everyone who makes the mess. Delegate jobs and have them share the burdens.

Some women think the children or the men should see what needs to be done and automatically do it. For this reason, they resent asking and end up doing the jobs themselves but grumbling about it, too. Think about this. Is it really logical? I have fallen into this trap myself. Many Moms seem to be the one to see all the work that needs to be done. Certain household members either don't see it or they see it and step right over it. Any likeness here?

When I ask my family to do a job: empty the dishwasher, take the garbage out, fold the laundry, feed the dog, take the dog out, do they do it? Certainly. Willingly? Yes. But do they do it *without* being asked? Sometimes but not usually. It requires a little more mental effort to ask, but at least it saves my physical effort for something else I need or want to do.

Stop doing it all and hire some outside help or start asking for inside help. *Will you please...? When you get a chance, would you...? Would you mind helping with..? I'd like to sweep the floor, do you think you could empty the dishwasher?* Get the picture? Don't order. Don't demand. Ask! With a please! Then follow up with a Thank You.

It's no secret that people want to improve themselves. Why, look at all the resolutions that are made on New Year's Day and other times as well. Resolves of everything from the practical to the philosophical. Resolves to lose weight, to quit smoking, to be kinder to each other, to be more gentle with the children, to be more thrifty, to work harder, to not work so hard, to have more patience, to worry less, to support more, to go but not to gad, to think, then act, to act not react, not to wish, but to set a purpose, not to complain but to be cheerful. To learn to say no because continually saying yes wears you down. To be grateful, to enjoy leisure but not a constant of it. To revel in the quiet, to be content. Striving at all of these and more are what keeps us going from day to day and week to week. Yet, said another way by another one (The Optimist Creed) perhaps will give you new thoughts for inspiration:

Promise yourself:

　　• To be so strong that nothing can disturb your peace of mind.

• To talk health, happiness and prosperity to every person you meet.

• To make all your friends feel that there is something in them.

• To look at the funny side of everything and make your optimism come true.

• To think only of the best, to work only for the best and expect only the best.

• To be just as enthusiastic about the success of others as you are about your own.

• To forget the mistakes of the past and press on to the greater achievements of the future.

• Promise yourself to wear a cheerful countenance at all times and give every living creature you meet a smile.

• To give so much time to the improvement of yourself that you have no time to criticize others.

• To be too large for worry, too noble for anger, too strong for fear and too happy to permit the presence of trouble.

If we succeed in accomplishing even one of these thoughts for the entire New Year, Bravo! But a year is a long time and most of us start off with a bang and end up with a mere puff, all of our good intentions gone by the wayside sometime during the year. So. Why not break the overwhelming 365-day resolution into a bite size piece, a single day.

Say to yourself: For this day only, I am going to follow a routine of trying to improve myself, regardless of the negative position I may find myself in. Then the next day do the same. Tackle your resolves to do better and be better bit by little bit.

Remember when going to a birthday party meant wearing your very best party dress and shoes? When going shopping meant wearing a dress and high heels? When going out for dinner or to a party meant really dressing up? These were special occasions and they called for looking your best.

Nothing has changed in that children still tend to be as excited about birthday parties. But their excitement wanes considerably when they are told to dress up. They see nothing wrong with wearing jeans to a birthday party. Not long ago, that would have been totally unheard of. Today, it seems to be a common occurrence.

Some adults don't even seem to differentiate between at-home clothes, running clothes and shoes and going-out clothes. Jeans and T-shirts have become the mainstay of the American wardrobe and the daily attire in school classrooms. Now, these clothes definitely have their place doing such things as maintenance chores, riding horses or bicycles, or washing the car. However, their place is not at parties, even children's parties. If the young people have this lasséz faire attitude, they will carry it into adulthood.

You know the old adage, people act the way they are dressed. Even Sylvester Stallone has said, "Clothes influence the way you feel." If dressed down, you will feel down, so manners will tend to be nil, as well. If dressed up, you will probably feel brighter, more cheerful, walk straighter, have more confidence and in general be more aware of how you act. Dressing down, in T-shirts and jeans or sweats, is really not a compliment to those who have invited you.

Not looking forward to a full two hours of waiting time once during a layover between flights, I decided to get some reading time in. However, I quickly abandoned this idea in favor of people watching. My mind wandered as I watched: Where were all these people going? Were others waiting for them? Why were they here? Was it pleasure? Was it business? Were they happy? Were they sad? Tall ones, short ones, large ones, small ones. Adults, children, men, women. Old people, young people. Handsome ones, not so handsome ones. Yellow skin, white skin, black skin, red skin. People traveling in groups, people traveling alone. Serious faces, smiling faces.

In all the differences that I observed, there was one common denominator. The majority held true to form: in their sweats, jeans, t-shirts and running shoes. Only a small handful of these hundreds of people were nicely dressed.

You could be doing yourself a favor by dressing up when occasions call for it. Looking good not only affects other people and their reaction to you, but can also enhance your own self-esteem.

Remembering names. At one time or another, remembering names seems to perplex most of us. On a daily basis we may come into contact with many people or we meet them at parties. Here are a few ideas to ease those difficult situations in which you might find yourself.

When being introduced to someone, listen intently for their name and say it immediately as you greet them. Repeat it in your mind several times, as well. If the person impresses you and you think you may be seeing them again, write the name down in a little notebook or on a file card when you get home and refer to it again.

This technique is good if you are a visual learner. Seeing the name in print will help you retain it. If you are an auditory learner, perhaps repeating it several times to yourself will be sufficient.

Everyone likes to be called by name, and people are even more impressed if you remember not only their name, but also an interesting connection about them (where they work, something they said or wore) and then mention that connection the next time you see them.

Try to find something unique about them and then relate it to their name. For example, Monica Pierce, with the piercing blue eyes. If it is a difficult name, practice it to yourself over and over.

Look for distinguishing characteristics that will help you remember the names and to whose faces they belong. It might be a hairstyle or an article of clothing, or possibly a clunky piece of jewelry. It could be a mannerism, a walk, a stance, a husky voice, a way they put their words together. Connect any one of these characteristics to the name, and the person will probably be indelibly etched in your mind. Another thought might be to associate the new name with someone you remember from your past. In any event, repeat the name to yourself.

Some principals, before school starts in the fall, memorize every name (particularly if it's a small school) going over each student's school picture. This takes some effort, but remembering names doesn't just happen. People usually work at it.

If your place of employment has a list of its staff or employees, go over it often, making mental notes of the faces. In your mind, place them in their respective offices. I've done this. It works.

If you belong to a club or organization, you might pull out your little notebook before your meeting or get-together and refresh your memory of the people you met there last. When you arrive and see them after some absence, you'll probably be able to recall the name from your list and connect it to the face. When you do, they will be impressed. More importantly, you will feel confident.

There was a place we went on vacation many years in succession. After two or three years, I realized that we were seeing the same faces. We had no contact whatever with these people during the year, so when we left our spot, their names also promptly left my mind. Until, one time, so as not to appear completely inept, I decided to jot down their names in my notebook with a distinguishing feature. As we arrived the following year, surely enough so did many of them. I had reviewed the notes on our flight and when I saw them I knew who they were and was able to call them by name.

If after all these attempts at trying to remember and your mind is still a blank as you encounter someone you've previously met, just be up front. Smile, extend your hand, and admit that you've forgotten. We've all been there.

Our choice of words and how we speak are among the ways we are judged by others. Pronouncing words correctly and using the right word at the right time tells people you are educated. Listening to people with good diction and a fine command of the language can be like listening to finely orchestrated musical numbers. Despite the fact that our language can be frustrating at times with many distinct uses and pronunciation of certain words, speaking well can be one of your finest assets.

In your effort to improve yourself, listen for the way words are put together when you hear good diction. It isn't necessary to use words beyond the normal range of understanding, but to add flavor and spice, be aware of and use verbs other than the usual variety.

When you hear new words, immediately pronounce them to yourself so you don't forget. Unobtrusively jot down words if you think you might not remember.

If you are shy about asking the meaning immediately, look it up in the dictionary at your earliest convenience and use it three times. According to experts, the word will then be yours. As you encounter new words in your readings, look up the meanings. This won't increase your reading speed, but it will enhance your vocabulary.

Good English grammar can be cultivated without much effort. Following is a list of the most frequently misused and mispronounced words:

All the farther - Say, "This is as far as I am going," rather than "This is all the farther I am going."

Allow and allow me - When offering your services say, "Permit me," or "Let me help you with that."

An invite - The correct and only word is invitation.

Bad, badly - "ly" is often incorrectly added to words used as adjectives. The correct response to "How do you feel?" is "I feel bad," not badly.

Between you and I - Between you and me is correct.

Between - Use this only when comparing two things. For example, "between us two." Use "among us three," when comparing three or more.

Can't hardly - double negative. Say 'can hardly'.

Congratulate - The word is not congradulate. The first "t" must be sounded.

Consensus - When you add "of opinion," it is redundant. Consensus means general agreement of opinion.

Dais - As in a raised platform and is pronounced with a long "a" sound, "dá-is," not "di-as."

Dentist - This so often becomes denist. Don't forget the "t".

101

Either - It is correct to use either an "e" or an "i" pronunciation.

Folks - This word should not refer to your family, rather it is used to refer to a people or a nation.

Fifth - Sometimes this is pronounced fith. Be sure to sound the second "f".

High class - Considered slang. Instead, use superior, excellent, distinguished when referring to something or someone of high quality.

House, home - These are two entirely different words and one should not be substituted for the other. You bought your house but you live in your home. You are "in the house" but you are "at home."

Itch, Scratch - Don't confuse these two. Itch is the sensation. Scratch is the action, however you may have a scratch on your arm. In this case the word is also a noun.

Kindergarten - Sometimes this is pronounced kini-garten. Be sure to sound the "der" syllable.

Leave, let - Do not interchange these words. Say "let me go," not "leave me go", but you "leave" a building.

Like - This is often used incorrectly as a conjunction when the word "as" should be used instead. Such as, "It rained everyday just like it did last summer." The correct usage is, "It rained everyday just as it did last summer."

Manufacture - Many times this is pronounced manafacture. Be sure to pronounce the "u".

Off - Never say, "I got if off of him" when you mean to say "I got it from him".

Pardon me - Incorrect. Instead, say "excuse me" or forgive me" or "I beg your pardon."

The reason is because, the reason is why - The correct wording is: "The reason is that..." Because and why mean reason and they are not needed.

Second - Don't forget to enunciate the "d".

Sophomore - Not southmore.

Sore - This does not mean angry. It is a description of how you feel when something hurts.

Strength - Many times this becomes strenth. Be sure to enunciate the "g".

Yeah - "yes" sounds more cultured.

When we speak too fast, there is a tendency to connect the sounds, which in turn twists their entire meaning. A foreigner trying to learn the English language would scratch his head in wonder at hearing these terms familiar to most of us.

Also in slurring, give me becomes gimme, going to becomes gonna, and let me becomes lemme. Pronouncing words correctly is a big part of making yourself understood.

So. If you want to sound like the educated person you are and if you want to make a good impression, slow down your speech and enunciate!

Improve your critical-thinking skills by stretching your mind. If you function solely in an area that's comfortable for you, eventually that safe zone diminishes. So urge yourself to work on tasks that are a bit more difficult than you would normally tackle. Play games or read books that make you think. Take a course you've been intimidated by up until now. Master it. These things might be difficult at first, but if you persevere and then succeed, you'll feel exhilarated. A wonderful step toward improving yourself.

Part Four

Stand-out Enhancers and Ways to Simplify

This section suggests many ways to spruce up your life and your surroundings so they are aesthetically pleasing. Many ways to make things easier on yourself and to make some of the drudgeries of day to day life more tolerable.

Collect things you like
Surround yourself with lovely colors
Greeting cards and how to use them
What to do with all those photographs
What to do with photograph of your house
What to do with your Christmas cards
Your own from year to year
Those that others have sent you
Use your good things - don't save only for company
Do things beautifully not only for company but
for yourself as well
How to punctuate various areas of your house
How to open mail
How to dress a table
What to do with your bed when you're not in it
Try a new adventure
What to do with ribbons
What to do with outside entryway
How to use candles
Coffee- not the usual
Paper doilies and how to use them
Houses with names
Party ideas
Special groups
Simplifying travel with small children

Many ideas and ways to uncomplicate your life so you can relax more

Henry David Thoreau says, "Our life is frittered away by detail...simplify, simplify!"

Start a collection, if not for yourself, perhaps for your children: decorative eggs, baskets, blue and white porcelain, bells, pretty miniature enameled boxes, porcelain thimbles, or music boxes. Even pigs or cows make fanciful collections. Collect something you love or something that holds a special meaning for you. One friend has the most magnificent collection of Santa Claus' I have ever encountered. Even store displays don't compete with her collection of more than twenty years. They all come out at Christmas and they all hold a prominent place in her house and in her heart.

Do you have a music box that you adore? My collection of music boxes get wound often and their wondrous sounds accompany me while I am changing sheets or putting make-up on or dressing, or dusting furniture.

If you have beams in your kitchen or family room, hang baskets from them. Display your collection of plates or whatever else you might have. Bring it all out and enjoy it.

When having guests, do whatever you can ahead of time: cooking, cleaning and grocery shopping or food preparation. This will allow you more time to spend with your guests rather than doing chores while they are there.

Preparing for guests. Before overnight guests arrive, you might want to spend a night in the rooms your guests will be in, especially if they are not used on a regular basis. By *using* them, rather than merely giving them a cursory look, you'll know immediately if these rooms are lacking any of the essentials your guests might need.

If possible, have two pillows available for those who prefer to read in bed, a book light or lamp and a clock. Also have handy some interesting reading material, a wastebasket and plenty of tissues. Fresh flowers and perhaps a bowl of fresh fruit are always a nice touch, too. Empty at least two drawers and freshen with scented drawer liner or sachets and make space in the closet with spare hangers for their use. An extra touch here and a considerate thought there is all it takes to be a gracious host, offering warmth and hospitality to your guests during and right up to the end of their stay. Their visit with you will surely be a special one they will always remember.

Do you sew? Make slip covers for your furniture and change the total look of your room with the season.

Frame your posters. If they're tacky, pitch them.

Do not allow a container of milk to ever make contact with your table unless it is in a pitcher. Same goes for orange juice or cream. Just the other day, our fourteen year old daughter, Mary Carol, had some friends over and they were snacking in the kitchen. Apparently they had asked her about our use of pitchers. So she said, "Mom, why do we use pitchers?" My response was that it was just a nicer way of living. One of my life enhancers. "Oh!" They all said.

Pamper yourself. Stand under a hot shower to take the chill off your bones. Treat yourself to a manicure or a pedicure. Even if no one sees your toes, this is to make *you* feel better. Have a facial or a lip, underarm or leg wax. Facials are wonderfully relaxing and rejunvenating.

Luxuriate in a bubble bath or put bath oil in your water. You bathe anyway. Surely you can afford five minutes to soak. Be sure to use a bath mat and a neck pillow. If you're unduly drained, try the aromatherapy on your pulse points: at your temples and behind your neck. Then soak in the water inhaling the scent. Does wonders to relax you.

Keep your nails neatly filed and manicured. If you can't afford a professional manicure and don't have time to polish your own, at least give them a coat of clear polish or lacquer. It dries quickly and adds a finished look. This goes for men, too. A coat of clear polish on a man's nails adds a note of elegance.

Tuck a nail file or emery board in your purse or even in the car. When you are kept waiting for any length of time, use the opportunity to touch up your nails.

Impeccable undies. Replace your lingerie at the first sign of wear. Refuse to wear anything with holes or runs. Do you wear only white? Be frivolous. Get lacy, colored or floral undies. Want sexy? Buy black. Wear a pretty nightgown. Keep your clothes in prime condition. There is no excuse for wearing stained, tattered or wrinkled clothing. Men, too!

Dress up when you go shopping or to appointments. Remember, you'll not only look better, you'll also feel better.

Energy begets energy. In other words, if you feel sluggish, lazy and tired, instead of going to bed, go for an invigorating walk.

Use accessories. Not all at once, of course, but earrings, pins, necklaces, or bracelets all help to enhance an outfit. An attractive saleslady in a boutique once told me she loved pins to the extent that at times she would wear five or six at one time! Not everyone could manage this, but she had style. If you feel you could get by with something like this, try it.

Drink lots of water. You may say you're not a water drinker. Neither was I. But since I've put myself in the habit I have found it to be quite refreshing. It keeps your system flushed. If you have a tendency to bloat monthly, curiously enough, you won't when you drink enough water. You *can* drink too much; don't overdo. Six to eight glasses a day is plenty. Water also keeps you filled and hopefully away from snacking. Sometimes I add a lemon wedge and sip it through a straw. Order it with lemon and straw in a restaurant, as well.

Surround yourself with and wake up to cheerful colors. Get your day off to a positive note. Use accessories to accomplish this. The quickest and easiest way to change the look and feel of a room is to change your pictures. Top selling accessory items include pictures, lamps and silk flower arrangements. If the lamp is still good, change the look by buying a new shade.

I almost pitched three very good lamps. The unattractive shades were so overpowering, that's the sum total of what I saw. Suddenly I realized new shades would make a difference. They did!

Short of gutting an entire bathroom, the right shower curtain and set of towels did the trick, instead.

Use a placemat and your best china and crystal even if you are dining alone. *Especially* if you are dining alone.

Once in awhile use cloth napkins even for your family. Buy remnants of fabric in your choice and cut them into squares. Then hem or pink the edges. Make them all alike or different, whatever suits you. Definitely use the cloth napkins for company. When you do use paper napkins, gravitate toward the heavier, better quality, even on a daily basis. Although there is the inexpensive kind, they are chintzy and nonabsorbent. I shy away from these.

Or for a party, buy fabric, pretty but inexpensive, and cover your tables with it. Buy all one print or mix and match florals with plaids or polka dots. Pink the edges or form the corners into knots. Or gather the corners with ribbons, then tie the napkins with same colored ribbon to coordinate. One hostess made a floor length tablecover, navy with pink flowers. She topped it with a lime green cover, tied the corners and napkins with pink ribbons and layed a pink rose (in its own water vial) across each dinner plate. Smashing is what it was!

Open your windows and drapes to let the gentle breezes blow through and the sun shine in.

Walls. Tired of plain, painted walls and can't afford wallpaper? Or maybe you'd like a different look. Try sponge painting your walls for a unique effect. Or buy one roll of your favorite wall paper and cut out the design. Then trim a doorway or around a window with these designs. Or maybe a border will give you the effect you want. Speaking of wallpaper, if you're wondering what to do with leftovers, I've come up with at least forty-five uses for it. (Check the back of the book for ordering).

Greeting cards. Instead of tucking into a drawer or pitching pretty greeting cards you've received, have them framed. Then enjoy looking at the beauty on your bathroom counter on an easel, or your bedside table or your desk. A friend of mine wrote a thank you note to me for a birthday card I'd sent her. This is what she said: "Dear Carol, Just wanted you to know how much I enjoyed your birthday greeting. The beautiful card graced my Baker's rack for weeks and is now a book mark."

Pretty papers. When writing letters or even jotting notes, do so on wonderful stationery or colorful notecards. Buy the blank cards and personalize your notes. Or personalize the blank cards on your computer. Then use them as invitations. If you hand letter, use colored ink of your choice or perhaps to match your paper. Use gold initial seals or colorful stickers. Check out the commemorative stamps at the post office. Buy the ones that most appeal to you instead of the "going" one. Match your ink color to the stamp.

Photographs. How often do you pull out your photo albums and just sit and browse through them? Probably not often, right? Want to enjoy your old photos on a daily basis? Reach for the scissor and start cutting them. Yes, you read right. Trim around the heads of each of the subjects and form them into a collage. Have it matted and framed to match your decor and it can be a focal point in one of your rooms and give you and your guests hours of pleasure at the same time. These can be made in any size: large or small and also make lovely gifts. (See back section for ordering collage instructions). One year I also made a family collage of snapshots to send out as a Christmas greeting when we couldn't get our clan together for a group picture. Another time, I placed a larger picture of the bride and groom in the center, and surrounded it with snapshots of the wedding, the bridal party and the reception, then presented it as an after-wedding gift to the newly weds, my brother and his wife. Still another idea. Ever wonder what to give as anniversary gifts to the couples who have been married for 25 or 50 years and really don't need anything new? How about this? Appeal to relatives and friends for special photos and combine them into a memory collage of years gone by.

House art. One day a young mother rang my doorbell. When I answered, her question was, would I like to have a pen and ink drawing of my house? *WOULD* I? Funny. I had been thinking of that very thing. A week later she presented me with a lovely picture of my house, matted and ready for framing. This artist thought she had no talent and was humbly surprised when I told her I wanted her to do another of my summer house on the lake. She did this one from a photo. The detail was exquisite. They looked professional and were elegantly done. Now, I asked her if she would take a short jaunt to the other side of town and draw a picture of the first house we lived in as newlyweds and new parents. I was absolutely enthralled with these drawings and they now occupy a prominent place in our current house. The wall, where the pen and ink drawings hang, tell a story of where we've been. It's a priceless tale that I'm reminded of whenever I look at this gallery.

Taking this one step further, I took the drawing to a printer which he copied onto the cover of a fold-over card. I created a poem for the inside and used it for the in-

114

vitation to a party. At the same time, I also asked the printer to run off some blank copies. Much to my delight, these I used for notecards.

Another wall in our house tells a precious story. For more than twenty years I created and designed my own Christmas cards, most of them with photos of the children. Some with photos of our entire family. All with verses especially chosen or composed by the children or me. The enlarged versions of these cards, the artist's art board from which he worked, are matted and framed and take up an entire wall from floor to ceiling. Creating and planning the cards was one of the highlights of my year. Some I planned years and months in advance. These all have a special meaning. They tell a wonderful story about us and are a wellspring of joyous memories I cherish each time I look at them. I derived great joy in the creation and I continue to feel immense pleasure by their very presence. Another exquisite enhancer to my life.

In the spring, go for a walk and pick a bunch of violets or Lily of the Valley. Tuck them into a small vase and put them where you will be sure to see them often.

Repetition makes a striking statement. Rather than one or two poinsettias here and there, try a cluster of four or five at the hearth or your entry way for a dramatic effect. How about several candles grouped together or a gathering of small objects? Consider a bunch of the same kinds of flowers in several different vases.

Use your china and crystal for yourself and your family. You may have lovely things you only take out for the holidays. You must own these pretty things because you like them. Start using them so you can have joy everyday not only when company comes.

If you work hard to do things beautifully for others, do the same for your family and even for yourself when you are alone.

Let your house waft with the wonderful smells of bread baking, spaghetti sauce cooking, cinnamon and spices simmering or apple pie baking. My husband is one who doesn't much enjoy the pleasures of eating. Yet, he loves to open the front door and come in to these marvelous aromas floating through the house.

Lace paper doilies. Use paper doilies on your plates or baskets as you serve cookies, crackers, cakes or anything similar.

More on doilies. Buy about a five inch diameter lace paper doily in the color of your bathroom. Drop it into the bottom of a clean wastebasket. European hotels do this as just another little extra to enhance your day. Though you might take a bit of razzing from friends and family, as I do, on this one.

Swing. Can you think of anything else as relaxing as sitting on a porch swing?

Make a statement. Wear a hat.

Line your drawers and cupboard or closet shelves with a garden of floral or scented liners. Something that suits your taste. But make it a joy for your eyes to fall into.

Store your bath essentials such as nail brushes, body brushes, loofah sponges and complexion brushes in a wicker basket near the tub. Even those unsightly shampoo bottles look better in a basket. Put another wicker basket for extra rolls of tissue near the commode if you haven't a cupboard or closet nearby.

Use an apothecary bottle or crystal decanter for your bath oils, colorful salts and crystals or even your mouthwash. An apothecary jar could hold your cotton balls, guest soaps or even pot-pourri.

Punctuate various areas of your house with lovely crystal bowls or wicker baskets filled with pot-pourri. Then enjoy the scents as you walk by.

Line your drive or walkway with clay pots of your favorite flowers.

Use a lovely letter opener instead of ripping an envelope open with fervor. Growing up, I always witnessed my mother opening an envelope with a knife. To my knowledge, she has *never* ever opened an envelope without using an opener. If you use envelopes that are lined with flowers or patterns, you need only seal the point of the flap. Easier to open, and the person opening the flap can also savor the beauty of the lining.

Set an attractive table. Use napkin rings. Practice elegant napkin folds. Use pretty colored or floral cocktail napkins. My friend, Terry, has crystal in glowing jewel tones. When preparing drinks, she matches the colors of the crystal and the napkins to the clothing of her guests. A unique touch. And fun!

Details may give the warmth you are seeking. Just the change you may need: Wallpaper borders, decorative shelf with collectibles, unique lighting fixtures, a change of cabinet hinges and door pulls, or maybe even a change in cabinet doors.

Try at least one new recipe on a regular basis.

Use garnishes to make your food look appetizing.

Keep the crumbs out of the butter.

Wipe around the tops of the ketchup and mustard jars before putting tops back on.

Buy soap and tissues in colors to match your decor, if dyes are not a problem to you.

Unique place cards. Use place cards at your dinner. Guests find them fun and they're helpful reminders if everyone is new to each other. But read on for some unusual ways of seating. Instead of names on the place cards have a food related item. Have guests draw the definition to that item and match it to the card. This is where they will sit. For example, Port Salut would be on the place card. The definition slip would say semi-soft cheese. Rotelle would be on the card. The definition slip would say small round pasta. Now, guests are not to cheat, but if they are positively stumped, you will have written the definition on the underside of the card. Get more ideas from your cook books.

Another hostess seats her guests according to whatever her dinner theme is. For Valentine's Day she has them draw the little hearts with messages on them and match them up to the heart at the table. Another great idea by one of our Girls' Supper Club hostesses: We drew raw pasta shapes from a small box and to find our place were to match them to the name of the pasta on the card at the table. For those who had difficulty, another pasta shape was taped to the inside of the fold-over card for a visual match. You could probably come up with lots of other ideas. Put your creativity to work. It's great fun and decidedly different from the usual name cards.

Your bed. Pull your sheets taut when making your bed. Ever the more comfortable than climbing into crumpled wrinkles. Freshen clean sheet ever more with a few sprinkles of baby powder. Every now and then spray your favorite perfume on the pillows and the sheets. Catch a hint of scent as you sleep. When he's away, try spraying his aftershave to keep him near you in thought.

Be daring and have a brightly colored lining sewn into your coat. Many years ago, Bill had purchased a lovely full length dress coat and I thought it might be fun to have a brightly colored kelly green lining sewn in. Being very Irish, Bill didn't need much persuasion. He thought it was a great idea. That's what we ordered, but when the coat arrived, we discovered, much to our dismay, a subdued, drab burgundy lining, instead. "What happened?" We asked. "Where is the kelly green lining we chose?" After a few phone calls and inquiries we were told the tailor thought there had been some mistake. No one in their right mind would have chosen such an obnoxious color for a lining to a dress coat so elegant. We insisted that there really was no mistake. Kelly green was what we ordered and kelly green was what we wanted. The tailor reluctantly changed it but that lining created more laughs, evoked more conversation and sparked more fun than some duddy old color ever would have. Had we settled for less, look at the fun we would have missed. Be plucky! Try a new adventure.

Relish the look of squeaky clean, sparkling windows.

Polish your brass and silver and enjoy the gleaming metals. On the other hand, some experts will tell you that "old" has character. People pay lots these days to make new look old. So if you have rusted urns or tarnished brass trays leave them "as is."

Ribbons. Use them generously for bows on packages, bookmarks, in your child's hair, around stuffed animals, around ceramic animals, to tie curtains back, around a potted plant, a book, a rolled up magazine, or a loaf of homemade bread. I've also made bows of red and white gingham or red tartan plaid and along with all of the other ornaments used them lavishly on my Christmas trees.

Coffee table books. Take them off the shelves. Invite them to be thumbed through and read by setting them out on your tables.

Your outside entryway. Make it say, "Welcome" to all who visit. Put a wreath on your front door. Change your door decoration with the season or holiday: A large red heart on Valentine's Day. A green shamrock or a very wide kelly green bow on St. Patrick's Day. A friend said she missed seeing all of our various holiday greetings on the door as she drove by each day, after we'd moved from her neighborhood. Find something that puts a bounce in your step as you approach your front door. Another friend placed a shallow container of large round lighted candles at her entryway. A delightful touch that said, "I'm glad you're here!"

A frog planter holds a geranium as he guards my entry. He also sports a whimsical grin. Puts a smile on my face every time I approach my own front door.

Candles! Indulge in them. They set a mood, create warmth, eliminate odors, are dazzling and spectacular and they can brighten, add pizzazz and bring cheer. Create a dramatic focal point in your summer fireplace. Arrange a striking display of twenty to thirty flickering candles and sit back and enjoy the glow.

Turn your lights down after dinner and escape to a place of soft candlelight, or to the glow of the hearth. Pamper yourself and bring some romance to your bath. Set up a cluster in your bathroom and relax to the warmth and shimmering lights, alone...or with him. Have a candlelight dinner and include the children.

Think of your patio as another room of your house. Entertaining outdoors? Add that pizzazz and dot it with candles after dark, or gently set floating ones in your pool. Line your drive with luminaries (lunch size bags filled with sand and votive candles).

On Christmas Eve, it has become a tradition in my town to border our front lawns and drives with these luminaries. They look wonderfully elegant. All over town.

Colorful tapers, votives, large round or folding columns all add up to an extra special touch and a bit of warmth.

Coffee doesn't have to be the same old day-to-day grind. Today's flavors and aromas are sensational. If you serve decaffeinated coffee to those who need it for health or sleep reasons, do freshly brew it. You could opt to serve some of the extraordinarily flavored coffees on the market today such as: Dutch Chocolate, Swiss Almond, Irish Cream, Hazelnut, or the myriad of others. Or, you could add a teaspoon or two of cinnamon as it brews. It is delightful. Serve accompaniments with your coffee: Whipped cream, chocolate chips, cinnamon sticks or flavored orange peel. Even if not for guests, give yourself a treat and add a bit of spice to your day.

Make one of his favorites for him: Vanilla pudding, yellow cake, lemon meringue or coconut cream pie when all you like is chocolate.

Loving house names. In days gone by in England, houses were proudly named by their owners. The house didn't have to be grand...just loved. I've lived in two houses with names and two with numbers. There is something ever so special about a house with a name instead of a number. Signs at the front gate and at the pier announced to all who approached that they had arrived at Orison Tryst, the name we gave our summer house on the lake. A poem by Francis Thompson, these words held a special meaning for Bill and me when we were married. Orison Tryst was a gracious lady, indeed, with an unexpected turn here and there and very much loved, at that.

Orison Tryst

Stand-out enhancers...Straight from the heart.
Have you ever gone above and beyond merely the basics? Consider this for a unique way of responding to others: My friend, Joan, came over one day when my children were very young. Unbeknownst to me, she had taken snapshots of each of them, then framed the photos in round wooden drapery hooks, she'd painted red. She added tiny, green velvet bows and presented them to me as a Christmas gift to be used as ornaments on my tree. Now, some two decades later, I still enjoy them on my tree and even though we are some distance apart geographically, they are a pleasant reminder of her. A delightful gift!

As a housewarming, relatives planned a surprise party in our new house many years ago. They arrived en masse with all the food and drink and even included a house gift besides. All we had to do was enjoy the party.

During that period of my life, when I was

124

housebound for a length of time, another friend went above and beyond the normal get-well greeting. In addition to several visits, calls, and meals, she presented me with a lovely basket filled with video movies, popcorn and a wine cooler. Now I could really lounge.

These kinds of behaviors are usually not touted in books. They are imaginative, creative and come straight from the heart. You surely know more than a dash of thought went into them.

Other examples of doing something a bit out of the ordinary:

❤ Snap a picture of the house of a special friend. Take that photograph to an artist. Then present your friend with a framed pen-and-ink drawing or a water color of the place they call home. Or have the photograph enlarged and framed.

❤ Keep a supply of children's gifts on hand. When your child receives a birthday invitation, no more last-minute shopping. It puts you in a better frame of mind too.

❤ When having a dinner party, wrap little gifts and use them as favors at each place setting for your guests to take home with them. Some ideas? A mini loaf of bread, Jezabel Sauce (recipes on p.152-153), or a jam. A refrigerator magnet, potpourri wrapped and tied in a square of fabric, a note pad, a mini plant. Things like that.

❤ After a large Christmas party one year, the hostess placed a vast wicker basket at her front door. In it were gingerbread cookies. On their way out the door at the end of the evening, guests were to take a gingerbread cookie home for each of their children. You can imagine their delight. Both the guests *and* the children.

❤ Another time we guests were given a Christmas stollen at the end of a holiday brunch.

❤ For a Valentine's Day Dinner, I made red fabric hearts, filled them with potpourri and gave them to the ladies.

❤ At another Valentine Dinner I'd had, I presented the ladies with small floral note pads wrapped in white paper and tied with red ribbon and the men were treated to a homemade loaf of strawberry bread. (recipes on p.152)

❤ For a Christmas dinner one year, I placed little Santas, their costumes all depicting a different country, on my table as part of my centerpiece. At the end of the evening, each guest chose her favorite one and took it home as a favor, a remembrance of the evening.

❤ If you are poetically inclined, write a verse for special occasions rather than buying a ready-made card. This goes for birth announcements, anniversaries, birthday and even thank you notes.

Keep in mind that whenever you bring a hostess gift to a dinner or large party, be sure to put your name on a gift tag. People begin arriving together and handing the hostess one gift after another. At the end of the evening, upon opening the gifts, she may not always remember which gift came from whom.

When friends are a priority, the words "too busy" never enter the minds of those who care. They just add one more thing to their already full list. These acts of kindness become automatic; a graceful response to any kind of happening. Simply nice gestures for and from nice people.

———⟫•◦•⟪———

Although the following ideas can be slightly expensive, if you can afford them, they will add a different dimension to an otherwise ordinary party:

❤ One warm summer evening, Bill and I held a large summer, outdoor gathering for our friends on the lake. We hired a caricaturist. She set up her spot on the lawn and the guests stood in line one at a time to have their caricatures drawn. Then they were given the drawing, as a keepsake, matted and ready to be framed.

❤ Music always adds a fun element when people are gathered together. That same evening, we hired a band and our guests danced to their heart's content under the stars.

❤ Another time, a pianist entertained us with Christmas Carols during a Holiday party.

❤ Bill is not a professional musician, but many times he will entertain at our small dinner parties with his guitar and singing. A nice way to cap off the evening.

❤ If you're the type who likes to prepare your own food for a party, but find that it gets to be a real job, try this: Prepare the items ahead of time, then hire professional help to serve the drinks, the food and take care of all the clean-up. To make it a little less costly, hire high schoolers who like to work in the kitchen. This way, you can be a guest at your own party.

❤ A marionette show was held for one of our

children's birthday parties and on another occasion, a clown entertained the children and for each of them shaped a long, thin narrow balloon into an animal figure.

♥ Our friends, Ginny and Doug invited their musician friends to a party once and on a very informal basis had everyone play their instruments. We sang and ate and had a great fun evening. Think of your own unique ideas as you plan your next party.

Secret sisters, a group of women who are given, by a chairman, the name of another woman in the group. That person is our secret sister for the year. We remember each other, secretively, with cards, gifts, notes, flowers or any little trinket we can think of during holidays, birthdays, anniversaries or just anytime throughout the year. In December, we have a Christmas Coffee and gift exchange at which time we try first to guess, and then reveal our names to each other. It's fun to receive unexpected gifts or deliveries at our door. Once my doorbell rang, but as I approached, no one was there. I stepped further onto the entryway and looked right, then left. My eyes fell on a young man running down the street. He never turned back but as I glanced in his direction, I also saw a gift perching atop the hood of my car. My secret sister's son made the "drop" for her, a silk floral arrangement. That incident put a smile on my face for the rest of the day and I chuckled whenever my mind replayed the scene. Our secret sister group has been a wonderful enhancer to my life.

Join a book group. Or start one. Ours meets once a month. We decide on what we will read, then we join together as a group to discuss the book. Many of us would not choose some of the books we read were we choosing them on our own. But with each one we read, we widen our scope, become a bit smarter, a tad more opinionated perhaps, even if it's knowing we never want to see a certain genre or read a particular author again. We alternate morning and evening meetings to accommodate those who work. Coffee, orange juice and breakfast type foods are served at the morning get-togethers. During the months we meet in the evening, we serve wine, appetizers, coffee and dessert. The end of the year is topped off with a spectacular Christmas party and we do have fun.

Another offshoot could be a movie group. Ours includes spouses. We choose a movie, current or video, and watch it at our leisure. Then we meet every six weeks for a Sunday night supper and a discussion on various aspects of the movie. All members take turns hosting and each couple brings their favorite dish to share, with the host and hostess preparing the entree. This, too, has been great fun. Some of the men balked and came reluctantly at first, but they eventually began to enjoy the gatherings.

Baskets or plastic dish pans are ideal for folded laundry. One for each child and another for Mom and Dad. Each person goes to the laundry room to get their own container or basket of folded laundry. A big simplifier and time saver for Mom.

Moving. As you remove pictures from your walls during a household move, remove the hook as well and tape it to the back of the picture. All you will need to locate is a hammer when you are ready to rehang the pictures in your new house.

Catalog ordering. When ordering from more than one mail order catalog, sometimes it is helpful to keep a chart to remind you what you ordered, when, from whom and how you paid for it (check or credit card). Check off that line when a particular item arrives. If it doesn't arrive in a reasonable time limit, you have your record to remind you to inquire about it. Also, all the pertinent information is handy if you need to return an item. P.S. Best to order by credit card. If problems arise, sometimes it's easier to cancel the order on your card than to get a refund.

When you have leftover pie pastry, but not enough for another pie, roll it out, sprinkle with cinnamon and sugar, and/or nuts if you like, roll up jelly roll fashion, slice on the diagonal and bake 350° 10 to 15 minutes or until done. Fresh, homemade, delicious cinnamon rolls. As a child, I looked forward to these every time my Mother made a pie. My children look forward to them every time I make a pie.

Mobile phone. As an adult, talking on the phone has not been one of my favorite things to do, partly because I felt glued to one spot and that I wasn't accomplishing what I wanted to do. But for times when I do get involved in a long conversation, the portable phones have saved me lots of frustration. I am able to walk from one end of the house to the other doing odds and ends: opening drapes, dusting furniture, tidying up, loading and unloading the washer and dryer, or folding clothes. If you don't have a portable phone, a 25' cord works well too.

Handy phone numbers. Instead of having to look in my file each time I make a phone call, I've typed frequently called numbers on an 8 1/2 x 11 sheet of paper. I've inserted this sheet in a sturdy see-through jacket (so it doesn't get dog-earred) and slip this into my caddy near the phone. I also list other frequently called numbers on color-coded index cards. For example, the children's friends' numbers (if I need to reach them in a hurry) is blue; Book group on a yellow card; and the home telephone numbers of several friends who work in the same office on a green card, all very accessible in a slot in the caddy. Rather than an address book, I have a card file. When addresses and phone numbers of various individuals change, I simply make a new card.

Coded keys. Car keys are usually easy to locate on a ring. But home and office keys are so similar that it helps me not to have to fumble if one of these keys is color-coded. Choose a colored key, or buy colored plastic rings to attach to the key to be able to see at a glance which key is which.

Familiar with the long handled car windshield washers in the filling stations? This makes a great window washer as well.

Measure cardboard, poster board or mat board to fit your drawers or cupboard shelves. Line the board with contact paper. No waste and easy to clean or take with you when you move.

When I transfer birthdays, anniversaries and other pertinent dates to my new year's calendar, I also include the date of any weddings we attended. Then I remember to send the couple a first year anniversary greeting.

Another simplifier: Address birthday and anniversary cards two or three months in advance, while watching television or during one of your "wait" times. Keep these on your desk or near your calendar with the date to be mailed either on a sticky sheet or in the upper right hand corner, to be covered by the stamp. You could leave the envelope unsealed so you can take a quick glance before mailing as a reminder of what you are sending or to add a personal note. This will save you precious time. When the date actually arrives, all you have to do is mail the card. You will have already spent your leisure time searching for the perfect one.

Company dinner record. So you don't serve the same meal over and over to your guests as they return to your house for dinner, it's helpful to keep a company dinner notebook with your menus, your guest list, and the dates you entertained them. There are lovely books on the market expressly for this purpose. Although, not as nice, you could also use a spiral notebook. The ever so popular blank books work well, too.

To get rid of the piles that collect and clutter, use files.

To save time, bathe two or three toddlers in the tub at once.

Food simplifiers and timesavers
• If your mashed potatoes are ready before your dinner is, simply cover the bowl with aluminum foil and the potatoes stay hot for many minutes. The same goes for baked potatoes.

• When you bake potatoes, bake more than you need for that particular night. Use the extras cut up and sauteed the next night.

• I purposely double my pancake batter so I have extras. Then I slip two pancakes in sandwich size baggies and freeze. They are very handy to pop into the microwave on busy mornings and are just as tasty. Same goes for French toast and waffles.

• If you like to make things from scratch, save yourself some time when making pancake batter. Measure all the dry ingredients and put them in a tin. When you are ready to make the pancakes, all you have to do is add the liquid ingredients. I've also done this with cake recipes.

• If you like toasted banana bread or muffins, a toaster oven is a great replacement for a toaster. It does the job of a conventional oven but on a smaller basis. You've now maximized your output and eliminated one small kitchen appliance.

• Whip heavy whipping cream the night before or several hours ahead. No need to do this at the last minute.

• Alphabetize your spices for ease in locating them. Or arrange according to category: Spaghetti sauce spices together, cinnamon, nutmeg and ginger together. Like that. Or store them at "point of first use". You know, baking items in a cupboard near the baking center and so on.

• Keep your cupboards organized and uncluttered. Face all labels toward you and keep all like canned goods together. You should be able to see at a glance what you have without moving every item.

• The same goes for the refrigerator. When it is so full that you have to remove half to see what is in there, it's time to condense. Pitch week-old leftovers and rearrange.

• After several leftover food items have accumulated and they say, "What's for dinner?" Tell them, "Mus'goes". "What are mus'goes?" They'll ask. Just answer: "Everything in the refrigerator MUST GO!" (Did I hear a groan?)

• Coffee is ready to serve all day at our house. To make it a pinch more attractive, I set the sugar bowl and creamer on a paper doily next to the coffee server with a colorful napkin to catch the drips.

My dining room table is unusually long and table-cloths are a problem. I either have to make them or I use placemats. My Mother gave me a lovely, old lace cloth that belonged to my grandmother, but as I proceeded to cover my table for a buffet I was serving, alas, it barely reached the ends. Rather than despair, I placed the palms of my hands on the center of the cloth and shifted it ever so slightly. Two of the corners hung slightly over the ends of the table and the other two corners draped down the sides of the table. Two of the table corners were covered and two of them were exposed. A decidedly different effect.

Clutter away! Keep your counters clear of things such as toothpaste, combs, brushes, makeup and similar such everyday items. Store the like things in a basket and/or put them in a drawer or cupboard. They'll be handy when you need them but not unsightly.

Travel hint. To simplify travel when our children were very small, I condensed our packing. Rather than lug seven suitcases, one for each of us, I packed a huge steamer trunk, instead. Hotel or resort kitchens are usually stocked with merely the basics. I wanted my own utensils. So. Into the trunk, I even tucked a teflon frying pan, my favorite can opener, my trusty coffee maker and, of course, there was room for a few of the children's favorite toys and any little extras to make our stay away from home more comfortable.

The story goes on. Then, I would send the trunk ahead. The hotel stored it in their trunk room until we arrived. For our flight, we would only take a few small carry-on items. When we arrived at our destination, we also didn't have the extra burdensome waiting time with small, tired children at the baggage claim. We disembarked from the plane and advanced directly to our hotel. A major plus, timesaver, simplifier, and headache reducer.

I recently came across this hint for another simplifier: Use one wrap for all occasions just by varying the color of the ribbon. For example: A red and white stripe or polka dot can be used for Christmas wrap with a green bow, on Valentine's Day with a red or white bow, for a springtime gift with a yellow bow, and for a 4th of July package, a blue bow.

Have a special center in your house where you keep gift wrapping supplies. I have had my center in my laundry room and in my basement. In my present house, I have a large armoire in my bedroom. In it are several large decorative boxes each labeled for quick reference: *Ribbons and Bows* (Scotch tape and scissors have their own niche in this box, too.) *All Occasion Cards, All Occasion Gift Wrap, Christmas Gift Wrap.* When it comes time for wrapping, everything is at my disposal and gift wrapping is not a frenzied activity of going to and fro looking for the proper tools.

Have pens and paper next to each phone for quick, easy message taking.

Be sure you have a good light by which to read.

Take a paper grocery bag with you to each wastebasket in your house, rather than empty each waste basket one at a time.

Don't fight looking for your eyeglasses, especially if you only need them for reading. I have five pair of inexpensive reading glasses: A pair in the kitchen, a pair next to my bed, a pair in my purse, another pair next to the chair I sit in most often and a pair at my computer. Saves anguish.

Storage systems for audio and video tapes and compact discs not only keep them free of dust but also keep them easily accessible.

Don't procrastinate. It's futile and it's a time waster. Break down overwhelming jobs into smaller tasks.

There are some people who intuitively know how to enhance the lives of others. Many people I know have this knack. They go the extra step. They have a flair for entertaining and an invitation to their house is always greatly welcomed. You probably know people like this, too. Every corner of their house, from the front door to the bathroom says, "I'm glad you're here." They and their houses exude a warmth and comfort that makes you want to stay and stay. And to top it off, they are guests at their own affairs. No, they don't have help. They do it all themselves, but make it look like they didn't do a thing. Take heart, though! Whenever something looks so easy, you have the full confidence of knowing that heaps and heaps of effort went on before you ever arrived.

Ralph Waldo Emerson says to "Scatter Joy". Joy being anything that causes gladness and delight.

Fill a candy dish with jellybeans and peanuts. Watch your guests scurry over their favorite colors.

Part Five

Reflections and Tidbits

This section of the book is mainly quotes by others, some famous, some not so. And the tidbits are those such as:

How to hold a wine glass
Where to store nail polish
Recipes for gift giving
Free pleasures
Facts of light
Things like that...
Pleasing or interesting
bits of information.

❤ "There is pleasure and beauty amidst order."

❤ "Most smiles are started by another smile."

❤ "Of all things you wear, your expression is the most important."

❤ "People are lonely because they build walls instead of bridges."

❤ "Happiness is not the absence of conflict but the ability to cope with it."

❤ "A thing of beauty is a joy forever; Its loveliness increases; it can never pass into nothingness."

Keats

❤ Ralph Waldo Emerson says, "Manners are the happy way of doing things."

❤ "There is no beauty so great as beauty shared."

❤ "We make a living by what we get, but we make a life by what we give."

❤ "The smallest good deed is better than the grandest intention."

❤ "Those who bring sunshine to the lives of others cannot keep it from themselves."

❤ "I expect to pass through this life but once. If,

therefore, there be any kindness I can show or any good thing I can do to any fellow being, let me do it now, as I shall not pass this way again." William Penn

💜 "There is no such thing as a free lunch." In every *getting* there is some *giving*.

💜 "When I want to speak, let me think first. Is it true? Is it kind? Is it necessary? If not, let it be left unsaid." Babcock

💜 *"Little words are the sweetest to hear; little charities fly farthest, and stay longest on the wing; little lakes are the stillest; little hearts are the fullest, and little farms are the best tilled. Little books are read the most, and little songs the dearest loved. And when nature would make anything especially rare and beautiful, she makes it little: little pearls, little diamonds, little dews. Agar's is a model prayer, but then it is a little one; and the burden of the petition is for but little; death is what remains of them all. Day is made up of little beams, and night is glorious with little stars."* Author unknown

💜 Excerpt of Barbara Bush's commencement speech at Northeastern University:

"Real tolerance is an idea that our country has strived for since its beginning. Certainly we've made progress, but we still have a long way to go.

How many of us have not shunned someone with a handicap because it makes us feel uncomfortable or made fun of a classmate for some real or imagined difference?

Tolerance is much more than just respecting people of a different race. It's a constant stream of little acts in our daily lives.

The Anti-Defamation League has reported that anti-Semitic incidents are at an all-time high and such incidents on college campuses have increased 35 per cent."

Mrs. Bush mentioned a letter she received during the Persian Gulf War from an Afghan girl whose Muslim family was harassed at their home in a northern Virginia suburb.

"Obscene words were spray painted on their front door, windows were broken, the tires on her father's taxi cab were flattened. This little nine year old girl was confused why a country who went to the defense of another half way around the world could be so rude in their own back yard?"

This Year "Mend a quarrel. Seek out a forgotten friend. Write a love letter. Share some treasure. Give a soft answer. Encourage youth. Keep a promise. Find the time. Forgive an enemy. Listen. Apologize if you were wrong. Think first of someone else. Be kind and gentle. Laugh a little. Laugh a little more. Express your gratitude. Gladden the heart of a child. Take pleasure in the beauty and wonder of the earth. Speak your love. Speak it again. Speak it still once again."   Anonymous

---

Just a thought. "The impression people get of your

man will depend largely on what you say about him and how you act toward him in public. Don't play the martyr or look for sympathy at the expense of your husband. If you make only favorable remarks about him and act as if he's a fine person, you'll be helping him as well as yourself."   Author unknown

In order not to warm white wine or champagne while sipping, the glass should be picked up and held by its stem rather than by the bowl. In addition, the color of all other wines is more able to be appreciated if the fingers are not covering the bowl.

Store candles and nail polish in the refrigerator. Candles will have a longer burning life and nail polish will go on smoother.

Take pleasure in the free things that surround us: the smell of freshly cut grass, the sunsets or the sunrises (if you're up that early). Watch the cloud formations and imagine the shapes they take. Listen to, do not just let them blend into the background, the birds chirping and singing. Stop and take delight in the laughter of children.

The sweetest thing to me in all the world, next to children laughing, is children singing. When Bill and I were planning our wedding more than two decades ago, our list included a children's chorus to sing at church. Glorious sounds come from children's voices.

Be aware of the light that surrounds you, whether natural or manmade. There is a direct affect on our moods. Lack of it tends to be depressing. If you have this tendency and you live where the sun shines rarely, turn lights on, not off, in your house.

In fact, according to Designers Gary Clark and David Smith of David Smith Ltd., Chicago, "Lighting is as important as other details, and it also makes people look better." So when you are thinking about your surroundings in relation to light, do as Smith and Clark did in one of their design projects, combine downlights, uplights, lamplights and even skylights to enhance your looks *and* the way you feel.

Do you react to certain situations that arise or do you merely *act*?

Do you look at your house as an extension of your personality and warmth or as an endless lifetime of drudgery?"

Consider this: The only thing that really seems to remain the same...is change. Read it again, if you will.

> **"Love is the Art of Caring**
> **Caring is the Art of Sharing.**
> **Sharing is the Art of Living.**
> **Living is the Art of Loving."**
> **author unknown**

Joy Whitman says: "After a while you learn the subtle difference between holding a hand and sharing a life, and you learn that love doesn't mean possession and company doesn't mean security and loneliness is universal.

And you learn that kisses aren't contracts and presents aren't promises, and you begin to accept your defeats with your head up and your eyes open, with the grace of a woman, not the grief of a child.

And you learn to build your hope on today, as the future has a way of falling apart in mid-flight, because tomorrow's ground can be too uncertain for plans, yet each step taken in a new direction creates a path toward the promise of a brighter dawn.

And you learn that even sunshine burns if you get too much.

So you plant your own garden and nourish your own soul instead of waiting for someone to bring you flowers.

And you learn that love, true love, always has joys and sorrows. It seems ever present, yet is never quite the same, becoming more than love and less than love so difficult to define.

And you learn that through it all you really can endure that you really are strong and that you do have value.

And you learn and grow with every good-bye."

THE SAYING OF OMAR IBN, AL HALIF, THE SECOND CALIPH:

"Four things come not back
The spoken word
The sped arrow
Time past
The neglected opportunity."

If asked, could you describe someone you'd briefly met, could you recall what they wore? How they looked? In a pressure filled situation, would you be able to describe an attacker or a burglar? Notice details. Not only on people but in all of your world.

Notice situations and take the humor out of them. Then relate the incident to someone else and share a laugh.

Change your routine. This could be effective if you are trying to kick a bad habit. For example, if you are trying to quit smoking and you enjoy coffee with your cigarette, change the places you frequent for coffee. Do things differently than you normally do in your effort to stop smoking or whatever. Try this: If you usually put your left shoe on first, put your right shoe on. If you wash the right side of your body first, try washing the left side. If you towel-dry your hair first, dry it last. It's amazing and even a bit curious what creatures of habit we are. I've tried this and have had a few chuckles over it because as I've changed my way of doing some of these very simple things, I've actually become confused as to where I am in my routine.The real purpose is to change some of your regular behaviors associated with your habits. Nevertheless, "Old habits perpetuate mechanical living." (Line in *Dead Poets Society*) Try it, if for nothing else, for a bit of self-awareness.

"What is REAL?" asked the Rabbit. "Does it mean having things that buzz inside you and a stick-out handle?"

"Real isn't how you are made," said the Skin Horse. "It's a thing that happens to you. When a child loves you for a long, long time, not just to play with, but REALLY loves you, then you become Real."

"It doesn't happen all at once," said the Skin Horse. "You become. It takes a long time. That's why it doesn't often happen to people who break easily, or have sharp edges, or who have to be carefully kept. Generally, by the time you are Real, most of your hair has been loved off, and your eyes drop out and you get

loose in the joints and very shabby. But these things don't matter at all, because once you are Real you can't be ugly, except to people who don't understand." *

And that's the essence of inner beauty.

———➤◆◀———

*From the Velveteen Rabbit by Margery Williams. Alfred A. Knopf Publishers.

Lessons From Geese

Author's Note: "Lessons from Geese" was transcribed from a speech given by Angeles Arrien at the 1991 Organizational Development Network and was based on the work of Milton Olson. It circulated to Outward Bound staff throughout the United States. I share it here with you, my readers, hoping we can all learn these lessons.

FACT ONE: As each goose flaps its wings it creates an "uplift" for the birds that follow. By flying in a "V" formation, the whole flock adds 71% greater flying range than if each bird flew alone.

LESSON: People who share a common direction and sense of community can get where they are going quicker and easier because they are traveling on the thrust of one another.

* * *

FACT TWO: When a goose falls out of formation, it suddenly feels the drag and resistance of flying alone. It quickly moves back into formation to take advantage of the lifting power of the bird immediately in front of it.

LESSON: If we have as much sense as a goose we stay in formation with those headed where we want to go. We are willing to accept their help and give our help to others.

* * *

FACT THREE: When the lead goose tires, it rotates back into the formation and another goose flies to the point position.

LESSON: It pays to take turns doing the hard tasks and sharing leadership. As with geese, people are interdependent on each other's skills, capabilities and unique arrangements of gifts, talents or resources.

* * *

FACT FOUR: The geese flying in formation honk to encourage those up front to keep up their speed.

LESSON: We need to make sure our honking is encouraging. In groups where there is encouragement, the production is much greater. The power of encouragement (to stand by one's heart or core values and encourage the heart and core of others) is the quality of honking we seek.

* * *

FACT FIVE: When a goose gets sick, wounded or shot down, two geese drop out of formation and follow it down to help and protect it. They stay with it until it dies or is able to fly again. Then, they launch out with another formation or catch up with the flock.

LESSON: If we have as much sense as geese, we will stand by each other in difficult times as well as when we are strong.

* * *

RECIPES FOR GIFT GIVING

Best Ever Banana Bread

1/4 lb. butter	2 mashed bananas
1 cup sugar	1 1/2 cups flour
2 eggs	1 tsp. baking soda
3 Tbsp. sour cream	1/2 tsp. baking soda
1 tsp. vanilla	Chopped nuts, optional

First, mash bananas. Then, cream butter and sugar. Add eggs one at a time, beating well. Add sour cream and bananas. Add rest of ingredients; mix well.

Double for two loaf pans, greased and floured. Or put batter into five mini loaf pans. Bake at 350° 45 - 50 minutes. Cool in pans 10 minutes. Remove when cool. Wrap in colored cellophane or cling wrap, tie with a pretty bow and present to a friend!

Strawberry Bread

2 cups strawberries (fresh or frozen)	
3 cups plus 2 Tbs. flour	1 tsp. baking soda
2 cups sugar	1 1/4 cups oil
1 Tbsp. cinnamon	4 eggs, beaten
1 tsp. salt	1 1/4 cups chopped pecans

Mix well: flour, sugar, cinnamon, salt, & baking soda. Blend oil and eggs, then fold in strawberries. Add to flour mixture, then stir in nuts. Sprinkle tops with a bit of sugar. Put batter into two greased and floured loaf pans or five mini loaf pans. Bake at 350° 45 - 50 minutes. Cool 10 minutes in pan. Follow procedure above for cooling and wrapping.

Carol Fitzgerald

Jezabel Sauce

1 (16 oz.) jar apple jelly   1 (16 oz.) jar pineapple
preserves
1 (1 oz.) can dry mustard   Black pepper, optional
1 (6 oz.) jar horseradish

Mix all ingredients together. Put in fancy jars and refrigerate. When ready to give as gifts, tie a ribbon around the neck of jar. Punch a hole in small card and tie it to the ribbon. On the card say: Jezabel Sauce - Top cream cheese with sauce and serve with crackers. Or can also be served with ham, grilled chicken or even egg rolls. Yum! (Keeps indefinitely in refrig).

✹ ✹ ✹

Spiced Pecans

1 egg white   1 tsp. cinnamon
1 Tbsp. water   1 tsp. salt
1 cup sugar   1 lb. Whole pecans

Beat egg slightly with water. Mix sugar, cinnamon and salt together. Coat pecans with egg white mixture. Put sugar mixture in large plastic container and shake pecans until all are evenly coated.

Spread out on cookie sheet and bake at 250° for 1 hour. Put in a decorative container or jar and give as a gift. A wonderful snack!

Candlelight Dinner Rotating Schedule
(Sample chart for one month)
(There are 15 couples in this sample group)

Hostess	Appetizer	Bread, Salad & Wine	Dessert	As Requested by Hostess
A	B	C	D	E
7	3	9	2	5
10	1	4	6	11
15	12	14	13	8

1. Make a master list and number all the couples in your group. Make a chart like the one above for every time you meet. If you meet six times a year, you will have six charts, all made out in advance, so everyone will know the schedule for the year. Label each chart with its appropriate month.

2. Give everyone a master list of names and numbers and a schedule of charts for the year. You will meet in groups of 8 to 10 (depending upon the number of people in your large group). One meeting a year could be as a large group.

3. Each couple will find their number on the master list. Then circle that number on each chart. The square in which they find their number: A, B, C, D, or E will tell them what category they are in. For example, the above diagram shows three groups. The A column is host/hostess and provides the entree for that period. Everyone under B brings appetizers. Everyone listed under C brings bread, salad, wine and so on. Also, depending upon the group size, you may only need four columns.

4. Reading the lines left to right will tell you who your host/hostess is and which other couples will be attending the same dinner. All you need to do is look at the master list and match names to numbers. At the end of the year, new groups are formed.

CONCLUSION

Dear Reader:

Well, there you have it. Short, sweet segments on how you can surround yourself with things that give you joy, and ways of giving, doing and being that bring you pleasure and make you feel good.

It has been my intention to share with you what has worked for me in the hope that you, too, will derive joy rather than drudgery in the myriad tasks in your daily life. Perhaps you will adopt some of my ideas. Perhaps my ideas will spark new ones for you. Whatever you have gleaned, I fervently hope has been good.

I am always open to new views and various ways of doing things that will simplify my life and at the same time make my heart happy. If you would like to write to me offering your comments or suggestions or to share new insights, I would be delighted to hear from you, and I will write back.

Mail reaches me at:

The Carobi Five Publishing Group
3106 Tamiami Trail North, Suite #275
Naples, Florida 33940

So long for now and thank you for reading my book.

INDEX

Part One 1
Much Ado About Being

Part Two 60
Preserve Your Sanity So You Don't Lose Your Mind!

Part Three 81
Move Forward So You Don't Fall Backward

Part Four 105
Stand-Out Enhancers and Ways to Simplify

Part Five 139
Reflections and
Tidbits

ORDER FORM

If you would like additional copies of this book, please fill in the blank below.

How Many

_____ Embracing Beautiful Moments............................$ 18.45 each

(Includes $2.50 postage and handling)

Florida residents please add 6% sales tax.

Other Publications Available by Carol Fitzgerald

_____ Etiquette for Children........................... (soon to be released)

_____ 15 Chicken Lickin' Choice Recipes

Easy, Elegant and Very Good ! ....$ 3.00

_____ 45 Uses for Wallpaper...$ 3.00

_____ Collage Instructions...$ 2.00

Total check or money order enclosed......................................$_____

Please make check or money order payable to:

The Carobi Five Publishing Group

3106 Tamiami Trail N., Suite 275

Naples, Florida 33940

Send books to:

Name_____

Address_____

City,State, Zip_____

Would you like the book autographed? If so, please print your name or the names of the persons to whom it will be autographed.

_____

_____

_____

(Please enclose an extra sheet if you need more space.)

ORDER FORM

If you would like additional copies of this book, please fill in the blank below.

How Many

_____   Embracing Beautiful Moments............................$ 18.45 each

                         (Includes $2.50 postage and handling)

                         Florida residents please add 6% sales tax.

Other Publications Available by Carol Fitzgerald

_____   Etiquette for Children........................... (soon to be released)

_____   15 Chicken Lickin' Choice Recipes

                    Easy, Elegant and Very Good ! ....$ 3.00

_____   45 Uses for Wallpaper..$ 3.00

_____   Collage Instructions...$ 2.00

Total check or money order enclosed......................................$_____

Please make check or money order payable to:

                       The Carobi Five Publishing Group

                       3106 Tamiami Trail N., Suite 275

                       Naples, Florida 33940

Send books to:

Name_____

Address_____

City,State, Zip_____

Would you like the book autographed? If so, please print your name or the names of the persons to whom it will be autographed.

_____

_____

_____

(Please enclose an extra sheet if you need more space.)